ONE ARROW LEFT

Caitlin Press Inc.
3375 Ponderosa Way
Qualicum Beach, BC V9K 2J8
www.caitlinpress.com

Text and Cover design by Vici Johnstone
Map courtesy of the Cariboo Chilcotin Coast Tourism Association (CCCTA)
Copy edited by Meg Yamamoto
Printed in Canada

Caitlin Press Inc. acknowledges financial support from the Government of Canada and the Canada Council for the Arts, and the Province of British Columbia through the British Columbia Arts Council and the Book Publisher's Tax Credit.

Canada Council   Conseil des Arts   BRITISH COLUMBIA   Funded by the   Canada
for the Arts   du Canada   ARTS COUNCIL   Government
                                                          of Canada

One arrow left : the memoir of Secwépemc knowledge keeper Cecilia DeRose / by Cecilia Dick
   DeRose ; with Sage Birchwater.
Dick DeRose, Cecilia, author.
Canadiana 20240460758 | ISBN 9781773861586 (softcover)
LCSH: Dick DeRose, Cecilia. | CSH: Secwepemc—British Columbia—Bigoraphy. | CSH: First
   Nations women Elders—British Columbia—Biography. | CSH: First Nations Elders—British Columbia—Biography. | LCGFT: Autobiographies.
LCC E99.S45 D53 2025 | DDC 971.1004/97943—dc23

ONE
Arrow Left

The Memoir of
Secwépemc Knowledge Keeper
Cecilia DeRose

by Cecilia Dick DeRose
with Sage Birchwater

Caitlin Press, 2025

Contents

Part 4

Married Life with Lenny DeRose— 95

Part 5

Empty Nesters and Later Years— 147

This book is dedicated to my parents Matthew and Amelia Dick, to my children DeDe, Sonny, David, Denny, Lulu and Wes, and to my late husband Lenny DeRose who stood with me through thick and thin over the 54 years of our marriage.

In particular, I dedicate this book to our many grandchildren and great grandchildren who all proudly proclaim their Secwépemc heritage and call me Kyé7e and Qné7e.

—Cecilia Dick DeRose

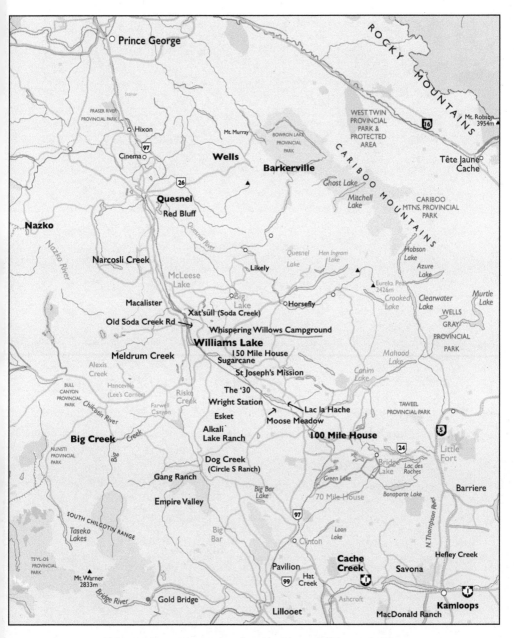

This map is representational and not intended for navigation.

Foreword

—Bev Sellars

Cecilia Dick DeRose has always been a part of my life. I knew her from a distance when I was growing up. She then became the Secwepemctsín teacher for my oldest son, Scott, when he was in high school in Williams Lake. He really liked her as a teacher.

I then got to know Cecilia as an individual when we hired her at Xatśūll to teach Secwepemctsín.

Later our community adopted Cecilia as one of our Elders.

She was so knowledgeable about so much of the culture because she lived it always.

Her knowledge did not come from four years in university. She has a PhD in culture and deserves to be recognized for her endless efforts to teach the culture and language.

She never said no and was everywhere spreading the word.

Introduction

—Sage Birchwater

I've been friends with Cecilia Dick DeRose for over half a century. We first met in 1973 in Williams Lake, where Cecilia and her husband Lenny were part of the close circle of family and friends of my neighbours Dave and Nene Twan.

Dave and Nene fondly recalled how they adopted Lenny as a young teen when he showed up by horseback at their doorstep in Narcosli, on the west side of the Fraser River between Williams Lake and Quesnel.

Lenny had a rough beginning in the small mining community of Wells, near the gold rush town of Barkerville, growing up without a mother. His dad worked all the time to support his three children, and Lenny, the youngest of the three, kind of ran wild in the community.

At fourteen years old, Lenny set out on horseback with two young friends to seek their fortunes. That's when Lenny got welcomed in by the Twans.

Cecilia is Secwépemc from the community of Esk'et (Alkali Lake), south of Williams Lake. She grew up with her loving and industrious family on a meadow near Lac la Hache, where she learned the value of hard work and the cultural ways of her people. Then, like most Indigenous kids in the region, she was whisked away to St. Joseph's Mission residential school near 150 Mile House at the age of seven. There she spent ten months of the year for the next nine years, until she "aged out" at sixteen years old and was turned loose to face the world.

Cecilia dealt with racism both inside the Esk'etemc community and outside in the broader society. Her mother Amelia Joe Dick was part white because her biological dad was a non-Indigenous ranch hand. Amelia was adopted and raised by her aunt Madeline "Met-len" Kalelst yet suffered unkindness from some members of the Esk'etemc community who never let her forget she was part white. They would call her séme7, Secwepemctsín for "white person," and refer to Cecilia and her siblings as sésme7, or "little white guys."

In the non-Indigenous society, Cecilia endured the prejudice directed toward First Nations people that included not being welcome to eat in public restaurants or find lodging in hotels, and being banned from attending "whites only" dances in the local Elks Hall.

Yet despite this adversity, Cecilia managed to connect with the core of her own goodness and inner well-being. She credits her father Matthew Dick for much of that. Matthew always insisted she remain proud of who she was and proud of her Indigenous heritage.

It was in Dave and Nene's household at Alkali Lake Ranch that Cecilia and Lenny first met. Cecilia was a sixteen-year-old graduate from St. Joseph's Mission residential school working at her first paying job as a housekeeper, and Lenny was a twenty-two-year-old ranch hand. Dave Twan was the ranch foreman in charge of hay production.

Five years later, on December 1, 1956, Cecilia and Lenny got married in St. Theresa Catholic Church in the village of Esk'et, and Dave and Nene were very much a part of the ceremony. Throughout the years Dave's name showed up repeatedly as a sponsor on baptismal certificates of Lenny and Cecilia's children, and the couple named their son David Joseph DeRose after Dave Twan.

When I met the DeRoses, they were living on a ranch along Highway 97 at 130 Mile, halfway between Williams Lake and 100 Mile House. They affectionately called their place "the '30" and had moved there in 1969 from Big Creek in the Chilcotin so their oldest child DeDe could attend high school. Cecilia had six children in six years, so DeDe's siblings soon followed her to Peter Skene Ogden Secondary School in 100 Mile House.

Before moving to the '30, the DeRoses had lived in numerous places across the Cariboo Chilcotin and Central Interior of the province: Alkali Lake, Dog Creek, Kamloops, Nazko, Quesnel, Meldrum Creek and Big Creek.

Lenny tended to be obstreperous. He'd start working at a place and get upset about something and then quit. But when he took the job at the '30 to manage the ranch for the Wright Cattle Company, Cecilia put her foot down and told her husband, "You can quit but I'm not leaving here until the kids finish high school."

And that's how it was. Two years after their youngest child Wesley graduated from high school in 1981, the Wright Cattle Company sold and the DeRoses left the '30 for Macalister, then Deep Creek, then to a place along the Old Soda Creek Road. Finally they settled in Williams Lake, where Cecilia continues to live today.

Around 1980, Alan Haig-Brown, the director of Indigenous education for School District No. 27, offered Cecilia a job teaching the Secwepemctsín language and Secwépemc culture in the high schools in Williams Lake. Cecilia was a natural teacher and continued in that capacity for nearly twenty years. She later went on to be a cultural educator in universities and provided expert advice to various levels of government.

Throughout all this time, Cecilia and I have remained friends. In the sparsely populated Interior Plateau region of British Columbia, and the ranching community in particular, friendships are typically maintained over great distances.

The DeRoses have long been a rodeo family. Cecilia's dad Matthew Dick loved to race his horses at the Williams Lake Stampede, Dave Twan was a rodeo star in his day, and Lenny DeRose won the steer-riding competition at the 1949 Quesnel Rodeo as a twenty-year-old and won the saddle bronc at the Williams Lake Stampede in 1955. Thirty years later, in 1985, Sonny DeRose, Lenny and Cecilia's oldest son, also won the saddle bronc at the Williams Lake Stampede.

In fact, all six of Lenny and Cecilia's kids excelled in rodeo. DeDe and Lulu competed in barrel racing, and the boys in rough-stock competitions. Sonny and David rode professionally in saddle bronc, and Denny was a professional bareback rider. Wesley was poised to turn pro in bareback in 1985, but his life was tragically cut short in the fall of 1984 at the age of twenty-one. The family created a high school memorial rodeo scholarship in Wesley's name to remember him.

⟫

In the early winter of 2023, a close friend of Cecilia's reached out to me, saying that Cecilia was ready to tell her memoir. For several months we recorded her stories and collected photographs; then she suffered a serious health emergency that threatened to end this undertaking. Miraculously Cecilia recovered, and we continued our journey.

In the spring of 2024, Cecilia's oldest daughter DeDe was named chancellor of Thompson Rivers University for a three-year term. Then, on June 4, Cecilia was awarded an honorary doctor of letters degree by the university. Serendipitously, this was DeDe's first official act as chancellor. "And that happened to be my sixty-seventh birthday," DeDe chuckles. "Mom thinks I set it up this way."

In her acceptance speech, Cecilia spoke as a parent, educator and knowledge keeper: "When teaching my six children and my students, I always told them we only have one arrow left. And that arrow is education. You must use it wisely, because we, your Elders, sacrificed a lot to ensure you have this arrow."

In our telling of Cecilia's memoir, it made sense to include the voices of her children. Lenny passed away in 2010, and Cecilia is the principal speaker throughout the book, but other speakers are introduced by name. Essentially Cecilia's memoir is a family narrative. Each of her children—DeDe,

Sonny, David, Denny and Lulu—adds a different perspective and unique recollection of events that only they can tell. These five strong individuals sometimes don't see things the same way and have differing opinions and points of view. But their voices add a richness and authenticity to Cecilia's story.

The common ground they share is a strong work ethic and a boundless love and respect for their mother. Cecilia turned ninety as this book neared completion, and she still lives in her own home in Williams Lake. And her kids want to keep it that way.

DeDe and Denny live in Kamloops, Sonny and David reside in Williams Lake, and Lulu lives in northern Alberta, but they all keep close tabs on their mom. The phone is a dial tone away and they all regularly visit Cecilia. They have also devised a strong support system that remains tight.

Denny, Lulu, Sonny, DeDe and David surround their mother Cecilia Dick DeRose at the 2018 Indspire Award ceremony in Winnipeg. All five children contributed to Cecilia's memoir.

This care and devotion is heartwarming, and deserved. Cecilia fought like a lion for her children and kept reminding them they had one arrow left: education. And her kids are indeed using it wisely.

PART 1

Early Life Before Residential School

1

The Beginning: Matthew Dick and Amelia Joe

I was the fourth of ten children born to Matthew Dick and Amelia Joe in the Northern Secwépemc community of Esk'et (Alkali Lake), about thirty miles south of Williams Lake along the Dog Creek Road.

I was born on January 14, 1935, and my midwife Louise Tom was the midwife for our whole village. The last baby she delivered was my sister Slug, nine and a half years later in September 1944. So my parents named her Margaret Louise in our midwife's honour.

My mom Amelia Joe was kind of an outsider at Esk'et. She was half white and half Secwépemc and people kind of picked on her because of that. But she acted more Indigenous than most Esk'etemc. People called her séme7 (the Secwepemctsín word for a white person or someone of European ancestry) even though she was Secwépemc. They never let her forget.

We had a house at Esk'et, but our main home was at Moose Meadow, about twenty-five miles away toward Lac la Hache. It took a day and a half to get there by team and wagon from Esk'et. That's where I mostly grew up. My dad ran his own guide outfitting business there and had hay leases on three meadows in the area. It was off the reserve, so he paid lease fees every year for those meadows.

My Mom Amelia Joe Dick

My mom's dad was a white man, Joe Smith, from Williams Lake. He was a ranch hand at Alkali Lake Ranch when he met my maternal grandmother Martha Williams. Later on, he married a white lady and had his own family. He became the local brand inspector and did that job for many years. Apparently he did acknowledge my mom, but I guess in those days you didn't see too many white-and-Indigenous marriages. A lot of white men left their Native wives and brought their white wives over from England or from wherever.

They named my mother Amelia and gave her the last name Joe because her dad was Joe Smith. My mom's mother Martha was working at Alkali Lake Ranch when she got pregnant with Joe. Charles Wynn-Johnson owned Alkali Lake Ranch in those days.

Mom was born on August 26, 1911, and her aunt Madeline "Met-len" Kalelst adopted her and raised her out at Gang Ranch. Met-len and her husband

Matthew Dick and Amelia Joe Dick at their cabin in Esket in September 1936 with their first four children: Victorine, five, Cecilia, twenty months, Martha, three, and Willard, four. Amelia is pregnant with their fifth child, Richard.

lived across the river from Alkali Lake next to Gang Ranch. My mother was their only child. So she grew up working like a man too.

At one time Gang Ranch belonged to Esket. Then in 1864 the owners of Gang Ranch took a hundred-year lease on that Esket land. When the lease came up for renewal in 1964, we never got it back. Gang Ranch managed to hide it, I guess. When the lease came up, they forgot about it. So we lost Gang Ranch. My mom was raised right there on the reserve next to Gang Ranch on the west side of the Fraser River. My mom's aunt lived there with her cows. The whole area once belonged to Esk'et, so we should at least get acreage back for it because my mom grew up there with all the Rosettes (Secwépemc members of the Stswecem'c Xget'tem or Dog Creek/Canoe Creek First Nation, who lived on the Gang Ranch side of the Fraser River).

Anyway, that's my story.

My mom had an older half-sister, Alice Jack, from her biological mom Martha and an older half-brother, Freddy Jack. Alice married Joe Belleau.

Met-len died tragically, murdered by her husband when I was little or before I was born.

Mom grew up working hard. My dad worked hard too. So we are hard workers here. That's what I want to put across.

My Dad Matthew Dick

My dad Matthew Dick and his brother Joe were identical twins born on April 16, 1902, at Esk'et. Their mom was Margaret "Makrit" Seymour and their dad was Dick Johnson. On their marriage certificate Margaret's name is written Marguerite but we always called her "Makrit," and we pronounced Seymour as "Simo." My dad and his brothers were given their father's first name, Dick, for their last name, because that was the way with the nuns and

Dick Johnson and Makrit Seymour Johnson holding their newborn twin boys Matthew and Joe Dick in 1902.

priests at that time. They always connected us with the father's first name instead of his last name. At Esk'et there were so many Johnsons anyway. So they took their dad's first name.

The earliest church records trace our dad's family to the early 1800s. His grandfather was Alexander Tlourtaskret Parkranaxt Johnson, born in 1843, who was the son of Parkranaxt and Shelinchatkwa.

Our dad's father Andre Dick Johnson Parkranaxt was born in January 1876. He was the son of Alexander Tlourtaskret Parkranaxt Johnson and Agatha Narachtetkwe Bestetkwe.

Dad had an older brother, Harry Dick, who later moved to the States, and he had two sisters, Clara and Cecilia, who both died pretty young. That's how I got my name, from my late aunt.

Dad also had a younger half-brother, Bert Johnson, who was born after my grandfather Dick Johnson died. I never knew my dad's dad, but I remember his mom Makrit. She was sickly in bed when we were little, so we had to play outside when we visited her at Esk'et because she didn't like us to be noisy. We were all in that house across from the church in Esk'et. The Dick house.

My mom's aunt Met-len owned the house we're in now at Esk'et. But my mom and dad had to buy that house back from the band after Met-len died. The band took it over and didn't allow the house to get willed to my mom.

That was Indigenous politics. They didn't like half-breeds. So my mom had to fight most of her life. She tried to prove herself as First Nations. She'd do her own hides, make her gloves and moccasins and all that, but no, she was still a half-breed to them.

My dad was a hockey player before he met my mom. In 1927 he played goalie for the famous Alkali Lake Braves hockey team that travelled to Vancouver to play the best semi-professional players down there. His nickname was the Man with a Thousand Eyes. His brother Joe might have played hockey too but he never stuck with it.

The Alkali Lake Braves Hockey Club

—Sage Birchwater

There's a historical photograph of the nine members of the Alkali Lake Braves hockey club standing on the grass of Victory Square in the heart of downtown Vancouver, British Columbia. The portrait of the nine men was taken by Vancouver Sun photographer Stuart Thomson in January 1932. It shows the dapper young Secwépemc men dressed in buckskin and cowboy attire, about to make hockey history.

Their opponents were the semi-pro Vancouver Commercials all-stars, also known as the Commerks, the best group of players assembled in the Lower Mainland. This was the first trip to the big city for most members of the Braves from the Indigenous communities of Esk'et (Alkali Lake) and Tsq'escen' (Canim Lake). They were the BC Interior hockey champions.

For the photograph, the hockey players are decked out in suit coats, sweaters and buckskin jackets. Some are wearing buckskin gloves, holding their cowboy hats and caps at their sides. It's a classic pose of cowboys from the BC Interior backcountry experiencing the province's biggest city for the first time.

The nine players are Joe Clemine, Pat Chelsea, Matthew Dick, Joe Dan, David Johnson, Alec "Sylista" Antoine and Alfred Sandy from Esk'et, and Louie Emile and Peter Christopher from Tsq'escen'.

They played their first game on January 15 to an impressive crowd of 2,500 at the Forum in the Pacific National Exhibition grounds. The game was so successful that a second game was scheduled five days later. This time it drew an even bigger crowd.

Though they didn't win, the amateur champions from the Cariboo held their own against the semi-professionals of Vancouver. What's impressive is that they were not blown out despite being outmanned. The Commerks had thirteen players and the Braves had only nine. One account of the two games says the scores were 4-1 and 2-0. Another version says the scores were 2-1 and 1-0 in front of eight thousand jubilant fans in the Denman Arena.

The undeniable truth is that the Alkali Lake Braves were experiencing a peak moment of excellence in their lives and hockey careers. They had become hockey legends.

The Alkali Lake Braves Backstory

Matthew Dick and the Alkali Lake Braves hockey club grew in prominence in the Cariboo and Interior of British Columbia after their inaugural season in 1927. At that time there was no official Cariboo hockey league, just a loosely knit organization of teams from Clinton to Prince George, including teams from the Indigenous communities of T'exelc (Sugarcane), Tsq'escen' (Canim Lake) and Esk'et (Alkali Lake).

As Irene Stangoe tells it in her book *Cariboo-Chilcotin: Pioneer People and Place*, the Lac la Hache club was considered the top team of the day. They were to be the Braves' first opponents. Rather than getting blown out by a huge score, the Braves managed to hold their own and lost only 2-1. They were a team on the rise. Stangoe says it was a tough go for the Braves, who had to travel to games by teams of horses pulling sleighs. They were usually accompanied by another couple of sleighs carrying fans and family. Of course, they had to camp out in winter on their way to wherever they were playing, and once they reached their destination they had to camp out again. But this was a lifestyle the Secwépemc players were used to.

Hilary Place grew up at Dog Creek, a community twenty-two miles farther south along the Dog Creek Road past Esk'et. He was just eleven years old when the Braves were taking on Vancouver's finest in January 1932. The games were broadcast over the radio, but the reception was scratchy and would fade in and out as he tried to follow the action.

The nine members of the Alkali Lake Braves hockey team at Victory Square in Vancouver in January 1932. Left to right: Joe Clemine, Pat Chelsea, Matthew Dick, Joe Dan, David Johnson, Alec Antoine, Louie Emile, Peter Christopher and Alfred Sandy. Stuart Thomson photo, courtesy of *The Vancouver Sun*, a division of Postmedia Network Inc.

"Just when you'd hear that Alkali was starting down the ice, the radio faded out and the results of the rush were lost in the static. The last big fade-out happened at the very end of the game. When we heard the final score, Alkali had been beaten by one goal," Place writes in his 1999 memoir, *Dog Creek: A Place in the Cariboo*. He notes sportswriters covering the series predicted a walkover by the Vancouver squad with scores of 15-1 or more. "So we Cariboo people were more than satisfied with the showing."

Place describes the rise of the Alkali Lake Braves from farmhands on a remote cattle ranch to regional hockey champions:

> Conditions under which they played are hard to imagine. In 1930 the Alkali Lake team was playing all around the Cariboo. We often heard stories about their games. A typical match at Williams Lake usually went something like this: The weather would be clear and cold, about ten below zero Fahrenheit (−23 C), and a game would be set for two o'clock Sunday afternoon at the open-air rink in Williams Lake.
>
> On Friday the Alkali boys were getting ready to travel. The old green-and-white uniforms bought for the team by William Culham Woodward, owner of Woodward's Department Store, had been checked over, patched and mended with loving care by the wives and sweethearts of the players.

Place explains how W.C. Woodward was married to Ruth Wynn-Johnson, daughter of Alkali Lake Ranch owner Charles Wynn-Johnson, who depended on the Braves players as a workforce on his ranch.

He writes that after a good night's sleep, the players set out at six o'clock on Saturday morning for Williams Lake. "This was no luxury trip. It was 35 miles with sleighs and teams of horses traveling three to four miles an hour. That meant ten to twelve hours exposed to minus 10 F weather, not counting stops for lunch and resting time for horses on hills." He says the caravan of six or seven players rode in three sleighs and several saddle horses. "A few wives and children and even a fan or two piled into the sleighs for the journey. By the time they'd arrive in

Williams Lake late Saturday afternoon, the sun would already be set."

Place notes how Indigenous people weren't permitted accommodation in hotels or eating establishments in Williams Lake in those days, so they watered their horses in the Williams Lake River that flowed out of the lake and shovelled the snow and pitched their tents for their accommodations over the weekend. Cecilia DeRose says her family used to camp next to the Williams Lake River Valley where Surplus Herby's is today.

Each year the team got better and better. Finally, in the 1930–31 season, they managed to defeat the perennial champions in Prince George to take the northern BC hockey title.

Irene Stangoe writes that Andy Paull, president of the North American Indian Brotherhood, invited the Braves to Vancouver to play the all-star commercial team in the Vancouver Forum. She says they were an instant success and drew eight thousand fans to the two-game series.

In a 2022 article for *Montecristo Magazine*, the writer Tom Hawthorn confirms the Braves were the guests of the Squamish Nation leader Andy Paull, an activist for treaty rights, a labour leader, a sportsman and the leader of a musical band. "It will be the Indians' night to howl, we hope, and we of Squamish will have a 40-piece band at the game," the article quotes Paull saying. "We hope to play our boys off the ice to the strains of *See, the Conquering Heroes*."

The Alkali Lake Braves in their green A.L. hockey jerseys purchased for the team by Charles Wynn-Johnson. Back row left to right: Joe Clemine, Pat Chelsea, Alec Antoine, Louie Emile and David Johnson. Front row: Peter Christopher, Matthew Dick, Joe Dan and Alfred Sandy.

"The main event did not disappoint for pageantry or thrills," Hawthorn writes. "The opening faceoff was conducted by Chief Joe Mathias of the Squamish Nation in ceremonial regalia. Paull's orchestra performed before the game and between periods."

As it turns out, the Alkali squad was badly outnumbered with only nine players compared with thirteen for the Vancouver Commercials all-stars. As it was, the Braves had to borrow two players from their neighbouring Secwépemc community of Tsq'escen' to fill their roster. Louie Emile and Peter Christopher of Tsq'escen' are wearing their buckskin jackets in the group photo of the team taken at Victory Square.

An added factor: The champs from the Interior were used to playing outdoors with snowbanks containing the playing surface. Playing indoors on artificial ice contained by boards was something new for them. Cecilia DeRose says her dad told her the Alkali players couldn't get their breath playing indoors like that. Perhaps the smoke from the prolific cigar-, cigarette- and pipe-smoking audience got to them.

Despite the challenges, the Alkali Lake Braves did really well, and it was an experience of a lifetime for the Secwépemc athletes.

Sylista: The Braves' Secret Weapon

An important part of the urban legend surrounding this event and the team has to do with their best player, Alec Antoine, better known as Sylista. It was said he was a Tŝilhqot'in orphan adopted by an Esk'etemc family, and he was so good he could have gone pro. It is purported that he was invited to try out for the New York Rangers of the National Hockey League by the club's general manager, Lester Patrick. But Sylista turned him down. He told Patrick he already had a good paying job making fifteen dollars a month at Alkali Lake Ranch.

Perhaps he realized he'd be a fish out of water venturing that far from home to the other side of the continent. As it was, most of the Alkali players had never been to the big city before and were wide-eyed at the twenty-storey buildings that graced the Vancouver skyline.

More Backstory

Several important convergences came together that allowed this special moment in hockey history to unfold.

Charles Wynn-Johnson, the owner of Alkali Lake Ranch, sponsored the purchase of the Braves' green uniforms with their "A.L." logos. His son-in-law Captain Laurie Wilson is credited with organizing and managing the team, with the help of Indian Agent Harry Taylor in Williams Lake. It is also said that professional hockey player Cully Wilson gave hockey and skating instruction to the Esk'etemc players.

According to Irene Stangoe, the Braves won one more Cariboo championship before bowing out of competition after the 1932–33 season. Their mentor Captain Wilson eventually returned to the East, and the Braves, without a coach and manager, quietly folded.

But by then the team had become a Cariboo legend.

And as far as Alkali Lake Braves goalie Matthew "Thousand Eyes" Dick was concerned, he had more important things to do: He was committed to raising his growing family.

Eighty-Two Years Later, the Alkali Lake Braves Are Honoured and Remembered

DeDe and Cecilia with the tribute Alkali Lake Braves hockey jersey worn by the Vancouver Giants junior hockey club in 2014. Photo credit: Sage Birchwater.

In a framed glass display case in Cecilia's living room, a hockey jersey with the Alkali Lake Braves logo and Vancouver Giants patches bears witness to another storied chapter of the Braves' colourful past. In 2014 the Vancouver Giants major junior hockey club celebrated the Alkali Lake Braves with a commemorative hockey jersey as part of a week-long Truth and Reconciliation event in Vancouver.

The jersey was created for the Vancouver Giants, members of the major junior Western Hockey League. Like many of the artifacts on shelves and cupboards around Cecilia's house, such as her berry baskets, buckskin moccasins and gloves, photographs, lard pails used by the kids for carrying water and other memorabilia, the hockey jersey has a story to tell …

DEDE: I was the superintendent for Aboriginal student achievement for the province of BC for two years, from 2013 to 2015. I lived in Kamloops and travelled all over the province helping school districts improve Indigenous student outcomes.

In the spring of 2014, the Truth and Reconciliation Commission was going across Canada interviewing all survivors of residential school. The site chosen for BC was the PNE grounds in Vancouver for a week-long event in September. One of the days was dedicated as a Student Day, when students from across BC would come and be a part of the Truth and Reconciliation process.

Murray Sinclair was the lead of the Royal Commission on Truth and Reconciliation, and I was part of the committee to set up this day-long thing for kids. Five thousand kids from across the province came.

At one of the committee meetings someone said, "Isn't it great that the Vancouver Giants are going to wear the Alkali Braves jersey at their hockey game?" It had just been decided and I knew nothing about it because everything was happening so fast.

I said, "Did I hear you right? The Vancouver Giants are planning to wear the Alkali Braves jersey?" They said, "Yeah," and I said, "My grandfather was the goalie for that team." They said, "No way!"

One of the organizing committee people for the youth day was overseeing the whole thing for the Vancouver Giants, so I said, "How do I get in touch with the organizer to get tickets? Because my mom is going to want to go to that game."

He put me in touch with the guy organizing it. I called the guy and he said, "I hope you're going to like the jersey."

I said, "Can you show it to me?" So he emailed me a picture of the jersey. Then I said, "Where can I buy them?" And he said, "You can't."

"What do you mean you can't?"

"We didn't make them to sell; we made them for the players to wear."

"Well," I said, "they must have made some extra ones."

He said, "Call this number and ask them, I don't know that."

So I called the number, and they made six extra jerseys, and I bought all six.

Then I called my brothers and my sister to find out who could go down to watch the game. Denny and Cam from Kamloops, my son Matthew, and Sonny and Tracy and their two boys all wanted to go. So I got them a block of tickets sitting together. Then I got them the jerseys. Sonny and Tracy drove Mom, and they got in right at the start of the game. They wore all six jerseys, and Mom was cheering and walking around with her jersey. She didn't know any of the players because she didn't follow major junior hockey, but she was cheering loud.

And she was so excited. She was yelling and a bunch of Esk'ets were there as part of the Truth and Reconciliation week, and they were all asking Mom where they could buy the jersey. And we had the only ones for sale.

I actually think Esk'et did get a couple of jerseys from the players after the game.

I got one goalie jersey and five player jerseys. I gave Mom the goalie jersey, and she made sure that Sonny's son Dylan got to wear it, because he was a goalie then.

Irene Stangoe, *Cariboo-Chilcotin: Pioneer People and Places* (Heritage House, 1994), 61.

Hilary Place, *Dog Creek: A Place in the Cariboo* (Heritage House, 1999), 71–72.

Place, *Dog Creek*, 67–68.

Place, *Dog Creek*, 68.

Stangoe, *Cariboo-Chilcotin*, 61–62.

Tom Hawthorn, "90 Years Ago, a Hockey Team of Indigenous Cowboys Took on Vancouver," *Montecristo Magazine*, April 14, 2022, https://montecristomagazine.com/community/90-years-ago-hockey-team-indigenous-cowboys-took-vancouver.

Stangoe, *Cariboo-Chilcotin*, 62.

2

Our Family: Early Days

My Dad Had the Eyes of a Hunter

No wonder my dad was such a good hockey goaltender. He had the eyes of a hunter. He could spot a deer or a moose before anybody else could see it.

We'd be riding along in the wagon and he'd stop. "You see that?" he'd ask.

You'd follow his eyes looking across the meadow. "See what? I don't see anything." You could spend half an hour trying to figure out what he was looking at. His eyes were just tremendous. I can't explain it.

"There's a deer over there at the edge of the timber, standing on the far side of the meadow," he would say.

I still wouldn't see anything. It would take you minutes before you'd finally focus on it. We'd get going again and something would move. A deer would start bounding away and into the forest. "Oh, there it is!"

His reflexes must have been pretty good too. He stopped all those pucks and didn't have any scars on his face. Goalies in those days didn't wear masks, so he must have caught all the pucks before they hit him.

My Parents Married in 1930

Both my parents attended St. Joseph's Mission residential school at 150 Mile House near Williams Lake. My dad was nine years older than my mom, so they weren't students there at the same time. But after my dad finished school, he worked at the mission ranching and haying, and that's when he met my mom. The mission had cows and horses, and everything there was team and wagon at that time. They didn't have tractors. Quite a few Native people worked at the mission over the years. I remember Pascal Bates worked there when I was going to school. His wife Phyllis worked in the kitchen and he worked on the ranch.

Mom was still attending school when my dad worked there. She graduated from school at sixteen years old, because that was the age they kicked you out of school. But she kind of hung around the mission for a while and worked there herself for a couple of years.

Then the nuns and priests decided my mom should marry my dad. She was sort of an orphan, because her Aunt Madeline, Met-len, who raised her, had died. So they picked my dad for her to marry. He was twenty-seven and she was only eighteen. They got them together, married them on February 1, 1930, and sent them off to have children.

It worked out, because they were married for over fifty years. In 1980 we celebrated their fiftieth anniversary at the mission because that's where they got married. My mom and dad had ten kids, but there are only four of us left today. Martha Sure, me, Spic (Julia Victorine) Alphonse and Slug (Margaret Louise) Gilbert. Martha is the oldest now.

Met-len's Tragic Death

Mom's aunt Met-len, who raised her, was killed by her husband. He strangled her. We're not sure what year it happened. I'm not sure if Mom was still a student at St. Joseph's residential school when Met-len died.

Whenever Met-len and her husband came down to the reserve from the family meadow, her husband always rang the church bell. So when he came down and rang the church bell, nobody got suspicious. And then my mom's relatives started wondering after he kept hanging around the village and Met-len never showed up. So they went up to the meadow and found her dead in their cabin. Her husband had strangled her and piled some hay in the corner of the cabin and set it on fire, but it went out. They got up there and found her body after he'd left her to burn.

Met-len was the one with the money. She was the one with the cattle herd. She probably was handling all the money, and he wanted to be the big shot. And she wouldn't let him.

DAVID: According to moccasin telegraph, the family took care of the injustice of Met-len's murder after the cops refused to look into her death. Everybody knew her husband did it, but the cops wouldn't press charges. One day her husband was cutting hay up on the meadow and someone shot him. And to top it off, they took his body into the cabin and tried to burn it down. But just like what happened when Met-len's husband tried to hide the evidence of her murder, the cabin never burned. So the evidence of what happened was plain for all to see, and they never did get the person who shot him.

Our Family

CECELIA: Victorine was our oldest sister. She was born in January 1931. But she was sickly with tuberculosis and never went to school. My parents didn't want to send her off to the Coqualeetza TB sanatorium in Sardis because Chilliwack was such a long way away. They didn't know if they'd look after her properly down there. At the mission, when you got sick they'd just stick you in the dorm and leave you there. I guess they didn't realize she could have got better. Their trust in the white man wasn't very high.

Victorine died when she was nine or ten years old. It was in the spring. I remember there was no snow on the ground when they buried her, but I was so young I can hardly remember. She died from TB. It's a wonder the rest of us didn't get it.

Willard was the next born, in August 1932. We called him Willet.

After him came Martha, born in November 1933 in Empire Valley. She later married Bill Sure. We knew her as Madda.

I was born on January 14, 1935. They called me Cil.

Richard came next on September 30, 1936. He was baptized Alfred Richard, but we just called him Richard. Secwepemctsín speakers couldn't pronounce the R so we called him Leech.

Irene was born on March 7, 1939. She married Tommy Basil in Cache Creek, and we called her Eileen.

Bernard was born on December 26, 1940, and his nickname was Bennett. We also called him Beans.

Spic (Julia Victorine) was the next one born, on September 12, 1943. Spic married Willie Alphonse at Sugarcane.

Slug (Margaret Louise) was born a year later on September 4, 1944. Slug married Willie Kobalt and then later married Rick Gilbert.

The nicknames Spic and Slug came from the way we described them. Spic, the Big One, because she was a year older, and Slug, the Little One, because she was younger. That's how the old folks called them, "Spic-a-one" and "Slug-a-one."

Last of all was Felix Noel, born on November 11, 1946. Our nickname for him was Belix. He was the first of our brothers to go. He got into a tractor accident in 1971. At twenty-four years old he was gone.

Our Hard-Working Family

Doing hay contracts, we were Dad's hay crew. Our family's only way of travel when I was growing up was with horses. Team and wagon, team and sleigh or by saddle horse. My parents never owned a motor vehicle. We hayed and we worked.

My dad had lots of horses. Team horses, saddle horses, racehorses and hunting horses. Before I was born and when I was very young, he'd do hay contracts for all the big hay places around, Diamond S Ranch, Circle S Ranch, Empire Valley, Gang Ranch and Alkali Lake Ranch. In fact, my older sister Martha was born at Empire Valley a year before I was born, while they were haying down there. They must have had a wet summer, because Martha was born in November and they were still down there finishing up the hay. Martha was born in a tent.

In those days it was all loose stacks. Our dad hired guys from the reserve with their own teams of horses to help with the hay contracts, and our whole family pitched in and worked together as well. As we got older, we were his haying crew.

I remember us doing the hay contract at Alkali Lake Ranch, before Spic and Slug were born. We used to camp beside the creek at the bottom of the hill below the reserve. Dad hired men from Esk'et to work on the hay contract, and my mom cooked for the haying crew. Laura Johnson helped our mom cook. She was married to Mom's half-brother Freddy Jack. Us kids helped out packing water from the creek for the kitchen. We had little lard buckets and we'd make several trips for water when they were cooking or doing the dishes.

Alkali Lake Ranch: A Brief History

—Sage Birchwater

It is said that Alkali Lake Ranch is the oldest continually run cattle ranch in British Columbia. Its origin can be traced back to 1861, when German-born Herman Otto Bowe pre-empted 360 acres of rich farming grassland at the head of Alkali Lake.

The ranch was established on what was then known as the River Trail that followed the Fraser River from Lillooet to Canoe Creek and on up the river to Fort Alexandria, as part of the brigade trail network that linked the various trading posts along the Fraser River to New Caledonia.

When gold was discovered in the gravel bars of the Fraser River in 1858, the River Trail became the main route north to the goldfields of Barkerville until the Cariboo Wagon Road was completed in 1863.

Bowe built a stopping house on his pre-emption to accommodate the steady stream of gold seekers using the trail. He originally called his place Paradise Valley. But on a hill overlooking the roadhouse, a white patch of alkaline soil could be seen by approaching travellers from far down the valley. At first the roadhouse was identified as "the place near the lake with the patch of alkali on the hillside." Gradually this name was shortened to Alkali Valley and the name of the lake to Alkali Lake. At some point Bowe's pre-emption officially became known as Alkali Lake Ranch.

Because of his reputation for providing good food and service, Bowe's stopping house continued long after the Cariboo Wagon Road following the San Jose Valley from Lac la Hache to 150 Mile House drew most of the traffic away.

However, the gold rush brought tragic consequences for the Indigenous people of British Columbia and the Cariboo Chilcotin, and the Esk'etemc were not spared.

During the fifty-year span of British Columbia's fur trade from 1808 up to the discovery of gold along the Fraser River in 1858, the verdant Alkali Valley was the uncontested homeland of the Esk'etemc and Northern Secwépemc peoples. The fur trade had served the interests of both the fur buyers and the Indigenous inhabitants of the land.

But the gold rush changed all that.

Overnight a flood of gold seekers invaded the once exclusively Esk'etemc domain, armed with a new set of rules and a mandate of conquest and colonization that ignored the well-being and best interests of the Indigenous inhabitants.

Essentially settlers were permitted to homestead and alienate land that wasn't directly occupied by Indigenous people. But these rules weren't strictly enforced. Furthermore the Esk'etemc occupied the whole of the land they moved about on seasonally. But this concept wasn't recognized or accommodated by the colony.

Esk'etemc knowledge keeper Phyllis Chelsea describes this push and shove between the settlers, armed with newly minted pre-emption certificates and land title deeds, and the Secwépemc inhabitants who persisted in occupying their ancestral homesites. "After Bowe staked his homestead, Esk'etemc families continued to camp on his pre-emption whenever he was away," Phyllis told me. "Old Mr. Bowe would chase the Indians away, and we'd keep coming back."

Phyllis says a standoff finally occurred when an Esk'etemc woman hid her walking stick under her skirt and pretended it was a shotgun. "She told Bowe she would shoot him if he didn't back off. That's why our village of Esk'et was established where it is."

In 1909 the Bowe family sold the historic Alkali Lake Ranch to Charles Wynn-Johnson.

Thirty years later, in 1939, Heinrich von Riedemann purchased the ranch from Wynn-Johnson for his son Mario and his family. The von Riedemanns had escaped from Austria just before World War II. In 1963 Mario's son Martin assumed ownership of the ranch until his death in 1975.

In 1977 the von Riedemann family sold the ranch to Doug and Marie Mervyn. In 2008 the Mervyns sold it to Douglas Lake Cattle Company.

Irene Stangoe, *Cariboo-Chilcotin: Pioneer People and Places* (Heritage House, 1994), 121

Barry Sale, "Haphazard History: Herman Otto Bowe and the Early Days of Alkali Lake Ranch," *Quesnel Cariboo Observer*, December 7, 2023, https://www.quesnelobserver.com/community/haphazard-history-herman-otto-bowe-and-the-early-days-of-alkali-lake-ranch-7283360;

"Historic Ranches," Douglas Lake Cattle Co., https://www.douglaslake.com/history-alkali;

Sage Birchwater, foreword to *Jacob's Prayer*, by Lorne Dufour (Caitlin Press, 2009).

3

Moose Meadow

Everybody at Esk'et had a little meadow. When I was young, most of the people in the village would move to their meadows a few miles out for the winter. That was the lifestyle. They only got together for Christmas and Easter, when the priests would come to the village.

My mom's family had a meadow fifteen or twenty miles up from Esk'et. They called it Clutulucwem, which means "Yellow Meadow" or "Yellow Land." We used to stay there once in a while when I was young. They'd trap and hunt squirrels and stuff like that. And my dad cut some hay there for our horses, but there wasn't enough to support two families because we had to share the hay with my mom's cousins and family. So it wasn't enough to bother with.

My dad and his twin brother Joe were guiding for Buster Hamilton over at Lac la Hache, and it was Buster who encouraged my dad to start his own guiding business. To do this, he needed enough hay to support his horses. So that's what he done.

⫘

Our dad and Uncle Joe got government hay leases on three meadows we called Moose Meadows, about ten or twelve miles from Lac la Hache. There was the Big Meadow; the Island Meadow, because it had kind of an island of rock and trees in the middle; and a third, smaller meadow. The rest was all trees and bush and rocks that went straight up from Lac la Hache.

To get in there we'd go from Wright Station at the north end of Lac la Hache, up past Dingwalls and Phililloo Lake. Our place was just on the other side of Helena Lake. Of course, once the logging roads went in there, it made it easier for us to get in and out. But it's straight rock back in there.

So Dad and Uncle Joe started their own hunting camp. They built a big cabin for their two families to share and another cabin for their hunters. And they built a barn and corrals for the horses and a ctsíllenten, or storage house. The cabin our families shared had a sod roof and we took turns staying in it. One family would camp out in the summer and the other family stayed in the cabin. But we'd all eat together in the house. The cabin was too small to accommodate all of us.

Uncle Joe had only three kids, Marvin, Andrew and Claire. But there were nine of us in our family.

Our dad had that guide outfit for a long time, until he got too old. Then he turned it over to my brothers. But they lasted only a couple of years.

By the time I was born, Moose Meadow was the main place we lived most of the time. Esk'et was lower down, so the grass was ready to cut there sooner than the swamp hay in the higher Moose Meadow country.

So Moose Meadows gave my dad and Uncle Joe the hay base they needed to feed the horses for their guiding business. They both apprenticed under Buster to become registered hunting guides.

After that, our dad just gave up our share of Mom's Clutulucwem meadow. He just let it go and set out on his own. Moose Meadow was off the reserve, so Dad and Uncle Joe had to pay lease fees every year. After a few years Uncle Joe left to go sawmilling around 100 Mile House, and Dad kept the leases up and paid the fees.

Uncle Joe was there maybe three years before the sawmills started opening up, so he just went sawmilling. His sons Andrew and Marvin were old enough to go sawmilling too, and so was my younger uncle Bert Johnson. Sawmilling was big money.

ᕯ

My dad's family also had a little hayfield in Esk'et. Tame hay. That was the Dick hayfield. He and his brothers used to cut it to feed our horses for the times we spent in the village. Then, once Auntie Alice lost her husband and didn't have anybody to cut her hay, she'd get us to cut her hay there as well. So we always had extra hay for the horses when we spent time in Esk'et.

When Uncle Joe and Uncle Bert moved to the 100 Mile area to go logging and sawmilling, we were the only ones cutting the Dick meadow and living there. So after we cut the Dick hayfields at Esk'et, we'd head to Moose Meadows to cut our hay up there.

We also had a huge garden at Esk'et that was mostly potatoes, and a smaller vegetable garden where we grew carrots, onions and turnips. Just the hardy stuff. We hardly spent much time at the village, but we had a house and root cellar there. We didn't have a fridge or electricity, so we had a hole under the kitchen floor to keep things cool in summer or to keep the vegetables from freezing in the winter.

The main root cellar was dug into the hillside across from our old house, and that's where we'd pile our potatoes, carrots, turnips and onions until we ran out. Several families had root cellars in the village at one time, but eventually there was just us with a big garden.

When we went to the meadow in the fall, we'd take two sacks of potatoes with us in the wagon and whatever carrots, onions and turnips we had left, and we'd store them in a hole under the floor of our Moose Meadow cabin. We'd run out of carrots early, but we always had potatoes and rice and beans.

We got flour by the hundred-pound sack, and my mom mostly made baking powder biscuits. We always had chickens. In my early years we had a few head of beef. My mom's aunt Met-len once had cattle down toward Gang Ranch. She lived at a place where they could cross the Fraser River. One year Met-len got the trophy for the best cattle herd when they brought the cattle to 150 Mile for the fall sale.

We found that trophy thrown over the bank at Esk'et. I don't know if Richard was cleaning the bank behind the house one year, and here was this trophy. She won for the best cattle herd. I guess they judged them by the herd in those years.

Mostly we lived off what we hunted or trapped. We had deer and moose and sometimes beaver and muskrat. We even ate squirrels once in a while. Chew on those little bones after we skinned them out.

We never had a milk cow. My dad didn't want to be bothered. Because then we'd have to have a cow tied to the wagon whenever we travelled. But we weren't big milk drinkers anyway. We drank coffee and tea by the time we got weaned.

My mom always kept chickens. When we moved from place to place, we'd haul the chickens in crates tied onto the wagon or sleigh as we went back and forth between Moose Meadow and Esk'et. So we always had eggs.

◢

My mom worked right alongside my dad. She was a hard-working woman. There wasn't such a thing as men's work and women's work. It all had to be done. And there were lots of us, both boys and girls in our family. We all worked as we got old enough to help out. None of us sat around. We done all the jobs haying. Anything the boys done, the girls had to do too. Except mowing the hay. Dad never let us women or girls operate the mowing machine. Just the boys done the mowing. Even my mom never mowed. She raked when we were little. But as soon as my brothers got big enough to rake, they did the raking.

So I guess there were gender-related jobs. My brothers never wanted to wash clothes either. They wouldn't even pack the water or heat it up for the laundry. That was "women's work." Just my mom and us girls had to wash them by hand. We helped the boys with their chores, but they wouldn't help us with ours. We had to do laundry ourselves without them, on rainy days or in between haying the meadows. Everything was by hand. Washboard and scrub brush.

🌾

On the hay crew my younger brother Richard ran the rake. Most of the time Martha and I would cock up the hay in the field in little stooks. Martha and I always stuck together. Richard would pitch on one side of the stook and Martha and I would pitch on the other side. The three of us would go together and stick a fork on each side of the stook and put it on the slip.

My brother Bernard drove one team pulling a hay slip. He was only about eight years old when he started out. Irene was about eleven, and she drove another team pulling a second slip. Each slip would get unloaded with my dad. The horses would get hooked onto the cables to pull the sling load up to the top of the stack. My dad would place it where he wanted, then trip the sling to dump it. Then he'd lower it down and we'd put the sling back on the slip and drag it back to the field with the team to get another load.

Making hay on a hot summer day, you really worked up a thirst. The younger kids who weren't old enough to work on the hay crew packed drinking water for those who were working. When Spic, Slug and Felix were little, they always brought drinking water to us in gallon jugs that our mom strung on each side of the saddle horn. They'd take the empty ones back and she'd refill them.

Amelia and Matthew with seven of their nine kids who made up their haying crew: Bernard, Irene, Felix in Martha's arms and Cecilia, with Spic and Slug in front.

The younger kids, Spic, Slug and Felix, brought water to quench the thirst of the older kids working on the hay crew with Matthew. Left to right: Cecilia, Richard, Spic, Slug, Martha, Felix and Irene.

Before we went to the meadow, our mom would buy a whole case of Freshie or Kool-Aid. People used to come around to the reserve and sell it, and we'd buy a whole case. When we ran out of Kool-Aid, we'd have cold tea or just plain spring water. Our mom would fill one of the jugs with water and the other with tea. Then Spic, Slug and Felix would bring them to us while we were haying. That was their job, the three of them riding on one horse.

We hayed and we worked. My dad always worked. When he wasn't hay contracting or cutting our own hay, he was guiding. Then in the winter he would go trapping at the meadow. My mother was lucky that way, because a lot of people sat on the reserve and pretty near starved to death. But we had a big family. And we worked hard.

Up at Moose Meadow there was just our family, because it was too rocky for everybody else. Except the meadows were nice and flat and the creek ran through it. So we were just all by ourselves up there. Just our family, and we could do our own thing.

We always had a sqílye, or sweathouse. Between the creek and the house was our sqílye. During hay season we'd have a sweat every second day. Otherwise we'd just swim in the creek in between sweats. The rest of the year, Mom made us sweat at least once a week. She'd say that when you wash, you don't get down to the dirt if you don't sweat it out.

Making Buckskin

Our mom was the hide maker. In the fall, when they hunted, she would scrape all the hair off the hides as they came in. She usually didn't finish them all at once. She'd get the hair and fat off, then hang them up to dry.

When she had more time, she'd resoak them and rescrape them and get all the extra fat and hair off. And then she'd soften it. Wash it in soapy water and twist and squeeze it. Then she'd put it on the frame and we'd take turns poking on it until it dried. The boys would help too. They'd take turns pounding on the hide once Mom got it strung up on the frame. Anybody who went by would poke away if they had a minute or two. It would be soft by the time it dried. Then she'd smoke it to the colour she wanted.

She taught us girls how to sew and make moccasins and gloves and stuff like that. And we'd help her with all that. She was pretty fussy. She'd make us do it over again if it wasn't done right. Like if the fingers were crooked, she'd make you undo it and resew it. Yeah, she was pretty fussy with her buckskin work. And she loved beading and using the fancy fringes. She liked beads and all that fancy stuff.

Other than the boys helping pound the stretched hide while it was drying, she did most of the hide tanning with us girls. And she liked it so soft that she could use an ordinary needle to sew her gloves and moccasins. Most people used a glovers needle with its three-sided point you could sharpen with a small file. She had glovers needles, though, which she'd use if the hide wasn't soft, and she'd sharpen them when they got dull. I had glovers needles too but I never bothered sharpening mine. When mine got dull I'd just throw them away.

So we learned to make buckskin just by watching our mom, then doing it with her. She'd have a nice smooth cottonwood scraping pole. She'd start out by cutting most of the hair off by hand, using a butcher knife. Then when it was down to stubble, she'd drape the hide over the smooth pole and she'd scrape it clean. Her scraping tool was an old broken scythe blade that wasn't good for cutting grass anymore. She'd get it razor sharp with an axe file or sharpening stone and put a handle on each end of the blade by wrapping the ends with some gunny sack or old pieces of buckskin so you didn't cut your hands.

She'd scrape it carefully to get that first layer of fat and skin off. The girls helped her, mostly, with the scraping. She made sure we didn't put any cuts in the hide as we carefully took the outer layers off.

She'd soak the hide in soapy water to get all the blood and fat out, then work the brains of the animal into the softened hide and let it soak for a couple of days. Every animal has enough brains to tan its own hide.

After rinsing it in fresh soapy water, it was time to start working the hide, pulling and stretching it back and forth until she could squeeze water through the skin. Just force the water through the tiny pore holes of the skin. Then she'd squeeze the water out by looping the hide around a fence post or small tree or something, tying the ends together and twisting it tighter and tighter using a small pole as a handle. Once we got it as tight as we could twist it, she'd hook the stick and let the twisted hide sit for a while. She'd cover it with a rag or something so it didn't dry out.

When it was ready to start working, she'd cut holes all around the edge of the hide and lace it to a pole frame with some thin rope. Once it was tight on the frame, it was ready to start pounding with her special hide-tanning tool, her stone-edged tképmen.

Our mom made her own tképmen by lashing a smooth, flat stone to the end of a four-foot-long handle. She'd have it all tied. The stone looked like a big agate rock that was split in half. One side was rough and the other side was smooth. Then everyone in the family took turns pounding on the hide and working it all day long until the whole thing was dry. The hide would stretch as we pounded on it, so she'd have to keep tightening the strings throughout the day, and we'd just keep pounding until it was nice and dry and soft. You just kind of lean on it with the tképmen and slide it. Push on it and slide it. You can't leave it half dried or it won't stay soft. So we'd all take turns pounding on it. That's what makes it so soft.

Then she'd take it off the frame and cut off the stiff parts around the edge where the lace holes are and smoke the soft buckskin to make it that yellow colour. The hide is white when you take it off the frame.

To smoke it, she was quite fussy. She'd use the rotten punk wood from a dead tree. She said you had to make sure there was no pitch in the wood, so we just used the punky part. She said if there was pitch in the wood, the smoke would make the hide stiff and hard to sew. Sometimes she'd use fir cones or pine cones to smoke her hides. But you had to make sure there was no pitch in them either. So they had to be dead, black cones.

As the hide was smoking, she would cover the whole thing with a tarp to keep the smoke in to get that nice brown colour. She'd keep checking for the colour because she liked the colour just so. Not too dark.

Hunting, Then Trapping

After we finished haying at Moose Meadows, our dad would get ready for his hunters. He'd guide them for a couple of months, then it would be time to start trapping for the rest of the winter. We'd go down to Esk'et for Christmas and then for Easter, then head back up to Moose Meadow again. After Easter we'd trap muskrat and beaver until the end of April or the beginning of May.

4

How Life at Esk'et Changed

Opening Up the Land for Settlers

That's what they done, they stuck us on the reserve and took the rest of our land. And then we couldn't go to school in a white school. They had schools for us to go to where there were nuns and religion and priests. We couldn't have our own beliefs. They figured our belief was heathen because we didn't have a god. Because their god was the only god.

When I was young most people in Esk'et lived on their meadows for the winter. That was the lifestyle. They only got together at Christmas and Easter when the priests would come. People didn't get to see each other very much, so they were glad to visit and celebrate with each other on these special occasions. Everybody would dress up and go to church. Men wore their fancy buckskin jackets and the women had their fancy shawls and handkerchiefs, and everybody went to church. And everybody prayed in Shuswap (Secwepemctsín). Except the Mass was in Latin. And everybody was happy to see each other.

But when they put the school on the reserve in the '60s, people had to stay in the village year-round to look after their kids, and they never went to the meadows anymore. That was quite a while after I was finished school at the mission.

When I was young we had a Chief or watchman at the village. Kind of a policeman who wandered about at night to make sure the kids were home and in bed. That was even before the drinking started.

There was no drinking when I was young. The drinking came in, I think, in the '60s, after I left school and after Lenny and I were married. The drinking came once Indigenous people were allowed to buy booze in 1963. That's when the trouble really came.

Before that they made homebrew and stuff like that, but they didn't know how to drink once they were allowed to buy it. The government disallowed it, then they allowed it. Then they had rules for whites and different rules for Indigenous people. In 1963 the government let Indigenous people into the pubs and bars for the first time, but they weren't allowed to take any booze home with them. So you had to drink it all right there and then go home. They'd drink too much, too fast, and they'd drink to get drunk. People would just come and get wine, but they had to drink the whole bottle and got drunk. So you had to fill up.

But we were lucky. My dad liked his booze when he could get around it, but my mom never did. My mom never cared for it.

But she made homebrew and she made moonshine, though she didn't drink it. She'd taste it to a point to make sure it was good. I think they used dried fruit or whatever to make the homebrew. I remember her with a bucket of ice and pipes running through it. And it was drip, drip, drip. And it was pure alcohol. Then she'd put it on a teaspoon and light it. She wasn't a drinker, but she had to make everything perfect. Her homebrew was the same.

You weren't allowed in the liquor store, so you had to learn to make your own booze. My mom never cared for it. But my dad, as soon as there was booze, he was right there. He didn't do it all the time. Just on celebration days. Even then, he wasn't always with the bunch. I think my mom kept him in line a bit.

5

Our Life on the Land

Thank God we didn't live close to town. We just came in every six months. But we had to camp out in Williams Lake. There were no buildings down over the hill, but there was a barn there and the owner would charge fifty cents a night for one horse. Most of the time we had three horses, because we had the team and my dad always had a saddle horse behind the wagon. We camped along the creek where Surplus Herby's is today.

We lived at both Moose Meadow and Alkali, and we'd come to town for our six months' supply of groceries. Flour, sugar, coffee, tea, beans, rice, macaroni and spaghetti. There was only Mackenzie's Store where the Fields store was later located. That's where the Cariboo Community Church is today.

We'd camp one night on the way coming in and hit Williams Lake and stay a couple of days. Then back home again, either to Esk'et or back to the meadow. We had to get our six months' supply because the store in Alkali didn't carry bulk supplies like Mackenzie's did.

In July the fish would be coming up the Fraser and we'd catch salmon in the river below the village. My mom would dry all the salmon we'd need for the winter. She'd store it on racks hanging from the ceiling of our ctsílleńten, or store cabin. We always had a ctsílleńten beside our house in Esk'et. And we had another one beside our cabin at Moose Meadow. Our mom would pack the dried fish into gunny sacks and store them on poles that were suspended from the ceiling by wires. She'd pack the sacks of dried fish on the poles so the rats and mice couldn't get them.

Most of the sacks of fish were safely stored away in the ctsílleńten, but she'd keep one sack hanging open in the house for eating. That way it was handy for us to get into if we wanted some "candy." Snack time. It was just like candy to us. Once the sack in the house was empty, she'd bring in another one from the ctsílleńten for us to eat from.

At Esk'et there were no bears to worry about, but at Moose Meadow the bears would break into the cabin if tasty food like dried fish or dried meat was left in there and not stored in the grub house. The ctsílleńten had a locked door and no windows they could break through.

Later on, we showed our mom how to can fish in a big tub outside. We kept the canned salmon in the root cellar at Esk'et to keep the jars from freezing. Our cabin at Moose Meadow and our house in Esk'et had a hole in the floor under the kitchen as a cool place to keep things in summer and as a small root cellar to keep things from freezing in winter.

🌿

We harvested kokanee from Lac la Hache in the fall when they were spawning at the end of September and early October. When they'd come into shore at Kokanee Bay to lay their eggs in the shallow water, we'd drag a net and scoop them out of the lake. Then we'd eat them fresh or my mom would dry them.

They were much smaller than salmon, but they were just as tasty. She'd dry them because we didn't have no freezers. So we'd eat them fresh or dried. We'd go down to the lake and catch and dry a bunch of kokanee in the fall, in between hunters coming and going or between haying the different meadows.

🌿

When we travelled between Esk'et and Moose Meadow by horseback with our team and wagon or sleigh, we'd take the road from Esk'et to Springhouse, then cut across to Chimney Lake and follow the road to Wright Station at Lac la Hache. The road to Moose Meadow left Wright Station at the north end of Lac la Hache and went in about ten or twelve miles.

Going from Moose Meadow to Williams Lake, we'd come out at Wright Station, then go up to Chimney Lake and on to Williams Lake from there. The route between Esk'et and Williams Lake mostly followed the existing Dog Creek Road.

Sometimes if we ran out of small things like coffee or tea at Moose Meadow, my dad would go by saddle horse to the store at Lac la Hache to buy a few necessities.

Berry Picking

We picked lowbush blueberries at Moose Meadow, and toward Horsefly we picked the highbush blueberries and huckleberries. There were always some raspberries up toward Horsefly as well.

When my dad went hunting up toward Springhouse Mountain, he'd spot highbush blueberries and he'd tell our mom about it. Then she'd load us up on horses and away we'd go with baskets on each side of the horse. I'd have one horse and Martha would have another, and we'd each have one kid in front and one kid behind. Our mom put Irene and Bernard with Martha, and Richard and Slug with me. Then my mom would have all the big berry baskets in front of her and one baby in a basket tied onto her. We'd all ride horses and go out to Springhouse and pick blueberries all day. We'd have a basket full of dried meat and dried salmon and homemade baking powder biscuits with butter for our lunch.

Most of the time our mom dried the blueberries because we didn't have freezers then. If we got enough, she'd make jam.

The kitchen in our house at Esk'et was an addition our dad built later on. So at Esk'et our mom would dry the berries on the roof of the kitchen, which wasn't as steep as the main roof. We had a ladder and she'd spread a tarp on the roof and put all the berries to dry on the tarp. Every now and again we'd climb the ladder and stir the berries around.

The cabin at Moose Meadow had a dirt roof, so we dried the berries outside on a homemade table. The top of our table was made with poles because it was too far to haul lumber up there. So we put the canvas across the poles and put the berries on top of the canvas.

Then we'd store the dried berries in gunny sacks. You always had flour sacks or sugar sacks. She'd store the dried berries in a sack and tie it to the ceiling in the ctsílleńten so the mice couldn't get at it.

Another important berry we picked was sxúsem (soapberry) for making "Indian ice cream." They were ripe in June or early summer, and we'd just place a tarp or cloth on the ground under the bush and shake the branches with a stick. Then you'd put the berries in a pan of water to clean all the leaves and sticks, which would float to the surface.

Sometimes we dried the sxúsem. My mom would smash them up and flatten them and dry them in containers in the sun until they were like fruit leather. Then, once they were dry, she'd cut up the fruit leather and store it. When she wanted to make Indian ice cream, she'd soak enough for one batch and whip it up. At first we just had a stick with rags or something on the end to whip it up with. We started with that, then later we had an "uptowner," a rotary egg beater. The sxúsem would foam up like beaten egg whites. You add sugar before you whip them up.

6

Guiding for Buster

My dad and Uncle Joe started guiding for Buster Hamilton at Lac la Hache before I was born. Buster was the brother of Rita Place, who married Hilary Place at Dog Creek, and Buster and Rita had Indigenous ancestry. Buster lived on the east side of Lac la Hache toward Mount Timothy, where the ski hill is today. When our dad and Uncle Joe were guiding for Buster, we'd camp right at his place.

Even after my dad and Uncle Joe got their own hunting and guiding area at Moose Meadow, they still worked for Buster when he needed them. Bernard was the baby of the family the last time I remember being at Buster's guiding camp. I don't remember after that. They might have guided for Buster after I started going to school at St. Joseph's Mission, I don't know. Bernard was born in December 1940, and he was walking the last time I remember being at Buster's. There's a picture of my younger brother Richard with a dress on taken in 1938. My mother kept all her sons in a dress while they were still in diapers. She didn't have her kids in pants until they were potty trained.

Our family would get to Buster's camp a few days before his hunters arrived so we could get our own meat for our family to eat while we were there. One time, in the middle of the night, the dogs started barking and raising heck. This was just before Buster drove me, Martha and Willard down to the mission for my first year of school. The dogs were raising hell but they wouldn't go close to our meat-drying cache. The next morning we checked our drying meat and the bear had packed most of it away. The meat had been hanging on poles under a tarp with a little smoky fire beneath it. Where the dogs had chased the bear there was a trail of dried meat all the way. We saw by its tracks that it was a grizzly.

The dogs didn't dare touch the dried meat on the ground. They were trained not to touch our human food unless it was given to them. Our dogs were good. They could have eaten that meat but they didn't. They weren't allowed to take our drying meat or fish and only took what we fed them. You could leave the food right there and they wouldn't touch it until you'd give it to them. And they weren't any special fancy breed. Just stray dogs. They were good-sized dogs. They'd lie right beside the food and they wouldn't touch it.

An example of Amelia's potty-training technique. Richard, standing next to Amelia on the right is wearing a potty-training dress. Violet Chelsea Belleau holds the horse with Martha, Willard, Marlene Belleau and Cecilia on its back. Norman and William Belleau stand next to their mom. Amelia is pregnant with Irene (born March 7, 1939).

Once Dad and Uncle Joe started guiding their own hunters, we had more horses, and us kids rode horseback any time our family went anywhere with the team and wagon or sleigh. As soon as we got old enough, we rode horses. There were usually five or six riders behind the wagon when we went anywhere. This was good for my dad because it kept the horses well broke for his hunters. He had to make sure he had well-behaved, gentle horses because some of these guys from the city weren't experienced riders.

We used to wonder how those horses stood for those guys from the city. It would take them forever to get on a horse. Then they'd take their pillows and tie them onto the saddle. I guess the saddle was pretty hard for them to sit on all day while they were hunting.

Dad had to get all the horses ready to go before the hunting started. They all had to be shod because of the rocky terrain back in there. He had his hunters all coming at certain times. One bunch would stay a week or ten days, then the next bunch would arrive. At most he took out four hunters at a time. Sometimes just two. He'd be taking one bunch down to Wright Station and picking up another bunch at the end of the lake there. He had it all organized and made all the arrangements for the hunts through the mail. He wrote his own letters. My mom wouldn't do it. She could read and write but she never did trust herself, so my dad wrote his own letters and made his own arrangements. We didn't have no such thing as a phone.

My mom wouldn't cook for the séme7 (white people) either, because they ate so fancy. They would have been happy to just eat whatever. But she wouldn't cook for them because she didn't think they'd want her Secwépemc-style food, which would have been meat and potatoes. They would have been happy. But no. She didn't want to cook for séme7. She thought they ate high-toned. She wasn't confident enough to feed them what we ate.

The year I started school we were camped at Buster's place and Dad was up the mountain guiding. So Buster drove me and Willard and Martha to the mission to start school. That would have been in September 1942.

Sometimes our dad would travel down to Washington state to line up hunters. He'd also attend big guide outfitter meetings. He never drove a car, so he'd catch a ride with someone or he'd hire somebody to take him down. He still got around even though he never drove.

He only went up to grade 4 at school, but he knew what he was doing. My mom made it to grade 6. Grade 8 was the highest anyone ever went in the mission. But most only went up to grade 4 or 5.

So my dad started his own hunting camp. He had that guide outfit for a long time.

Dad's hunters were good to us. They'd bring their wives' discarded fancy clothes they no longer used and give them to us. They were from places like Pasadena, California, and we'd dress up like fancy city slickers from Los Angeles on the reserve. Martha in particular liked to dress up fancy. But I always wore jeans.

One time Martha put on all these fancy clothes but was having a hard time walking in the high heels. So Richard got a saw and cut the heels off those fancy shoes for her. But that didn't work because then her toes were pointed straight up and she still couldn't walk in them. Richard spent hours trying to cut those hardwood heels off. But it was all for nothing. It was so funny. The toe came way up and wouldn't go down.

Trapping

We didn't have a trapline like a lot of families at Esk'et did. The Indian agent gave certain families traplines, but my dad and uncles never had one. So they had to kind of just trap wherever. Like up at the meadow was nobody's trapline.

Pierro Squinahan's trapline kind of went up into Moose Meadow country. Pierro was my dad's brother-in-law. His first wife, Clara, was my dad's sister. After she passed away he married his second wife, Lilly Johnson. Once in a while Pierro would come up and trap, but most of the time he let my dad and Uncle Joe trap there. But then Pierro quit coming. So we just sort of took over the trapping and hunting at Moose Meadow.

When the sawmills came in, Uncle Joe built a shack down by 100 Mile House, and he and his family lived there. So it was just our family up at Moose Meadow most of the time. We mostly trapped beaver, but there were lots of squirrels and muskrats and a few weasels and mink. I think they got the odd marten but not very often, and maybe the odd coyote.

Of course, once us kids started school we were never up at the meadow in the winter. So we kind of lost touch with the way of life we knew there as kids. With trapping you had to be patient. Uncle Joe was the competitive one. He'd go out there and try and catch the higher-priced fur like coyotes, lynx and cougars. He was more ambitious than my dad, and he liked doing the harder stuff. My dad did the easier stuff you could make money at, like muskrat and beaver and squirrels. But Uncle Joe liked doing the big stuff.

Joe was a happy-go-lucky guy. He loved people. My dad was the quiet one. And Uncle Joe was the people person.

PART 2

Life at the Mission

7

Leaving Home and
Heading to Residential School

Willard was the first one to leave home, at eight years old, and go to residential school at St. Joseph's Mission. That was in 1940. Then Martha was next, in 1941. They were gone for ten months, from September to June, and I remember being so excited to go pick them up when it was time for them to come home. We'd pick them up, then hit the stampede.

Once Willard and Martha were both at school, I was the oldest kid still at home. So I was responsible for my younger siblings Richard, Irene and Bernard, who was the baby at that time. And I had to help with the chores like washing diapers and all that stuff.

I was six years old when Martha left for school, and soon I was anxious to go to the mission too, because you get tired of babysitting and washing and rinsing all those shitty diapers. And they had to be sparkly white because my mom was washing them. I remember that. So I was kind of responsible for the younger kids.

When Martha finally got home ten months later, I asked her what school was all about. I wanted to know what she had learned and what they did. She just told me they prayed a lot. "You go to Mass and pray as soon as you get out of bed. You have to jump out of bed and kneel beside the bed and say your morning prayers. You learn a lot of prayers," she told me. "You learn a lot about God and stuff. Then when you go to the classroom you have to read the Bible. Then they explain the Bible part."

As the time drew closer for me to head off to school for the first time, I was getting pretty excited. Somehow I thought life would be easier at the mission than babysitting and looking after my younger brothers and sister. There was no end to the work preparing bottles, washing and changing diapers. Looking after them was no fun.

So in early September 1942, my mom had made all our clothes on her hand sewing machine for us to wear for heading off to school. Martha and Willard had only been home from school for two months, and now it was time for them to head back. This time I got to join them. Our family was living in a tent at Buster's place at the bottom of Mount Timothy, east of Lac la Hache, and my dad was up the mountain guiding for him. So the three of us climbed into Buster's truck and he drove us from Lac la Hache to St. Joseph's Mission.

ᾄ

There's no way I could have been prepared for what I was about to go through. We didn't have freedom at the mission like we had at home. We prayed a lot, that's for sure. They got us up at 6:00 a.m. and we crawled out of bed and knelt beside our beds to say our morning prayers. Then we had to make our bed perfectly and get washed in time for Low Mass at seven every morning from Monday to Saturday. And it was all in Latin so nobody knew what anybody was saying.

High Mass on Sunday was even more intense and went on for a whole hour. Sometimes I fainted in the middle of it and they would have to pack me out. They never did figure out what caused my fainting spells. I would just come to and had to carry on. There was no sympathy that I remember. To this day I have a phobia of crowds and people. I get the feeling like I'm running out of air. My bedroom door has to stay open, and when I go to bed I need a night light.

In church the girls had to wear a tam or cap. During the week we wore our everyday uniforms we made ourselves out of old army and navy pants. Then on Sunday we wore our "boughten" fancy uniforms. They were navy blue pleated skirts, and we wore a white shirt with them. They were our Sunday uniforms because we had to be dressed just so for church. Just so for God.

8

Cruelty at Residential School

So the mission was a rude awakening.

First of all, we were gone from our family for ten months of the year. And this went on for the next nine years. And some of the nuns and priests were very cruel.

As soon as we got to the mission, we had to put all our home clothes away in the attic, and we were each given a number and a bundle of clothes that we had to wear while we were there. Then we were deloused with coal oil. We had to put it all through our hair and put a towel on it overnight. Then our hair was washed and cut short.

My number was thirty-five, and that was my identity for the next nine years. Everything I owned had the number thirty-five on it, from the time I entered till I left. And the nuns weren't all that friendly. It was more like an army camp or prison. And we sure prayed a lot, and lined up a lot.

Students, priests and nuns at St. Joseph's Mission near Williams Lake.

My grade 1 teacher was Sister Cecile, and my first big trauma erupted on my first day in class because I was left-handed. That was a no-no. The work of the devil! I couldn't believe how hard it was to switch from left to right. That big ruler got me so many times left-handed. I must have learned, because I still write with my right hand today.

Then my teacher called me "chatterbox" and "long tongue," so I had more problems along with just being left-handed. I got the ruler so many times, I'd automatically duck when she came by my desk. I spent a lot of time in the corner with my hands on my head because I was chatting or whispering or forgot to use my right hand again.

Then one day she got me good. Whacked my left hand and sent me to the corner. With the ruler still in her hand, as I went to go to the corner, she pushed me. I tripped because I didn't want that ruler on my head, and I fell and hit the side of my head on the desk. I saw stars and got disoriented for a while. But I still had to go to the corner. I tried so hard not to cry. But I was the work of the devil.

Then my ear started to run. Pus was running out of it, and I went to the sister in charge of the medicine room when she opened up at 3:00 p.m. Sister John the Baptist was a nurse, and she syringed my ear and packed it with cotton batting. That was it. No questions were asked, but she must have known. My hair was all matted with the pus, but we were only allowed to shower once a week. So I was pretty sore all around my ear.

Yeah, and I'm still deaf in that one ear. It was running with pus all winter. I would wash it and the pus would run down. Sister John the Baptist kept putting cotton batting in there, but it would fall out and the pus would just run down the side of my head. She'd just clean it out, put stuff in there and put cotton batting in there. That's all they done. They never called the doctors. But we never saw a doctor at the mission.

Later on, they had a doctor for the Indigenous people that used to travel to different reserves, and he used to come to the mission once in a while to check kids' ears and stuff like that. That was after my ear quit running and I went deaf. So I'm deaf on this side.

🔖

But it didn't end there. When we got caught speaking Secwepemctsín, out came the strap! I don't know how we ever learned English. The nuns all spoke French, so our English to this day is not great. The question I always ask: How come they could speak French and we couldn't speak our Native languages?

It seemed like they just disliked me. That's how I felt. I tried so hard to get them to like me, but no, they had their favourites—the ones who spoke

English and looked white. And these were the bullies and tattletales. So we couldn't get away with a thing. They used to wait outside the candy store and take our chocolate bar or orange away, because one of the bullies would have her bodyguard there and she'd say, "Give it to her or I'll beat you up." Lizzy Bob, a big husky girl, was the bully's bodyguard. They even took our snacks away, our midday snacks.

Monday was laundry day. I must have been nine or ten years old. Maybe eleven years old. As juniors we had to wash the boys' socks, the girls' stockings and handkerchiefs. The yucky stuff. Snot rags and socks full of toe jam, because we only changed our clothes once a week. Now kids change two or three times a day.

The wooden washtubs were along the wall, and everything would be soaking with a scrub board in each tub. We just had to scrub whatever tub we were assigned to. So tub number one was mine and I went there, and it was girls' sanitary napkins, the bloody ones.

I went to Sister John the Baptist, the nun in charge, and told her I didn't have my period yet. So it didn't seem fair I should have to do that job. She just told me no talking back. Just do what was assigned for me to do. That was the lowest blow of my entire life, and the abuses seemed to come daily.

I got the job done, because it had to be white when I got done, with no stains left. After I wore my knuckles to the bone, the top parts of my palms were blistered. I gagged and puked, but I got it done. We were never allowed to talk about moon times. It seemed to be a sin of some sort. Nobody talked about it. I didn't know what was coming when I got it.

9

Our Parents' First Visit

My mom and dad came to see us just before Christmas. They were coming from Moose Meadow to Alkali, and they swung by to visit on their way to Alkali for Christmas.

I was so happy when I spotted their sleigh by the cabin at the end of the boys' yard. I was so overjoyed it's hard to explain. We couldn't wait for recess to come so they could visit us in the girls' parlour. I looked forward to visiting with my brother Willard too, because we were never allowed to talk to the boys or visit while we were at the mission together. The boys were in one part of the mission and we were in another section.

But while we had a good visit with our parents, we were kind of shy for the first while. Then we relaxed and started visiting. But we sort of had a guilty feeling. We had to be careful what we said. Our parents stayed two days but we only visited them at recess time. And Willard wasn't allowed to visit with our parents at the same time as Martha and me. He came up to the girls' parlour to see them after we had gone because the boys didn't have a parlour.

Before they left, our mom and dad left us two dollars each with the nun in charge of the candy store. And before my mom left, she told Sister John the Baptist that I had St. Vitus's dance, also known as Sydenham's chorea, a neurological movement disorder—a kind of nervous sickness similar to Parkinson's where your arms and legs move involuntarily. So Sister promised her she'd attend to it, and my parents left.

You'll never experience a worse sadness than to be deserted. That's how I felt as my parents headed away. It just left me feeling so sad for days.

After Christmas I was sent to bed because my disease was getting so bad I couldn't write or keep my arms and legs still any longer. So the devil got me again. I prayed harder. Told God I'd try harder to be real good and pray lots. Which didn't help much because I was always in trouble.

It got so I couldn't walk. I had to wait for my sister Martha to come with my meals and help me to the bathroom, and she would feed me three meals a day because I couldn't keep my hand still enough to feed myself. It was a tremor like Parkinson's that way. From Christmas to Easter I was in the big dorm, right in the corner next to the chapel.

The nuns' bathroom was just two beds away from my bed, but I wasn't allowed to use their bathroom. One day I really had to pee. So I attempted to make my way to the girls' bathroom myself, about fifty yards down the room. I started out going from bed to bed where I could rest and go again. I made sure I didn't mess the beds along the way when I'd sit on one here and there.

Finally I got to the bathroom. But it had a step down. I was able to make the step by grabbing on to the bathtub, one of those old-fashioned high ones, and I started for the toilet. But I didn't quite make it, and my pee went all over the floor.

I knew I had to clean it up but I was so exhausted. This was about nine or ten in the morning and lunchtime seemed forever away. My mind said, "Clean it up," but my body said, "No." But eventually I started working on it. I put my towel down to soak it up. Then rinsed the towel. It was a slow process. Turn the tap on and off. Eventually I just left the towel soaking in the water and left it for my sister. She was all I had.

Then I attempted the long journey back to my bed. I almost made it. Then one bed before my bed I fell. So there I was lying on the floor with no way I could get up. Finally I just lay there and waited for my sister to come at lunchtime. I thought I was going to die before she got there.

She came and helped me back in bed. But by the time she came, I was too tired to eat. My bed was always messy and food splashed all over. Crumbs and stuff. So it was pretty smelly. When the time came to change the sheets, Sister John the Baptist came and took my temperature and gave me a little white pill, smaller than an Aspirin. And maybe she'd come again in the evening.

But what got me most was those nuns Sister Laurence, who never smiled, and Sister Gertrude. They were mean and they were Irish. When one of them would come to use the nuns' bathroom during the day, she would stand by my bed and say for the umpteenth time that God was punishing me for whatever I had done. Or she'd say, "You're putting it on. Be still." So I'd try my hardest to be still and keep the involuntary arm movements from happening. Every time that chapel door crashed open, I'd try and pretend I was asleep. Sometimes I wished I would just die.

I lost a grade that year, and I never wanted to go back to the mission again. When my parents picked us up at the end of June with their team and wagon, I was so glad to see them. What seemed like such a hard time before, looking after my younger brothers and sister, was nothing now. I wasn't in a big hurry to head back to school after that. And it felt so good to be doing all the things we did together as a family during the summer. All too soon it was September and time for us to head back to the mission again.

If we were ever late getting back to school in the fall, like if we were still haying at Moose Meadow after a rainy summer, the Indian agent would send someone out from the rez to tell us that they would send the cops if we didn't show up soon. They'd threaten us and send a rider up there to tell us to get back to school.

⚑

Brother Collins was another story. We would have to bring shoes to him to be mended and he would say, "Bring them right here." Then he'd try to grab us and pull us to him. He'd say, "Come closer, it's okay." But that scared the heck out of me and I hated that chore. So the next time, I'd just throw the shoes on the floor and leave. He was kind of disabled and walked with a cane. He couldn't move very fast, but he always had that wicked look.

Two girls I remember the most were Lila Billy and Annie Pascal from Canoe Creek. They ran away when they returned in the fall, and their hair was cut short and they were strapped on their bare bums in front of all of us. They stayed in the same dorm I was in and they had to wear a gunny sack. I don't remember for how long. So I got the message. There was no way I was ever going to run away. Getting the strap on the hands was bad enough. But there were other runaways.

10
Daily Life and Education

The food at the mission was never that great. We had to eat what was served. We were given a dose of castor oil every morning, squirted into our mouths from an oil can. We learned how to work, and work hard. Cleaning, cooking, running the treadle sewing machine, mending clothes and darning socks.

We'd have different chores in the morning before school. Some had to clean the sinks. Some had to clean the toilets; there were six or ten toilets at the back of the room. Some had to do the floors, and some had to wash the windows. We had all kinds of chores to do. Sweep floors, polish floors. They didn't have fancy linoleum. It was that straight brown stuff where as soon as something lands on it, you would notice it. So you had to have it sparkling all the time.

They changed your chores every week. Some had to do the wood. They had big pieces of wood for the three furnaces downstairs. Two of us worked together to fill up the furnace every so often. Go down and stick wood in. There were two people for each chore.

LULU: When Mom was in St. Joseph's Mission, one of her jobs was going to the basement with another girl to feed the big wood furnaces down there. Before they finished their supper, her workmate told her, "Don't eat all your bread." When they got down to the basement, the girl went back behind the woodpile and brought out a big can of honey from where she'd hidden it. By the time the week was over, they had to finish up that big can of honey or get found out. Mom said she didn't want to even look at honey for a long time after that.

CECELIA: There were fifty-four girls when I started school. Then it worked up to sixty, and then in Spic and Slug's time there were seventy-five girls. But most of the years I was there, we had between fifty and sixty-five girls.

We went from 9:00 a.m. to noon in the classroom, then in the afternoons you worked from 1:00 to 3:00 p.m. Monday was laundry day, Tuesday was ironing day, and on Wednesday and Thursday you done sewing and mending. And we made our underwear from flour and sugar sacks.

For one of the sewing projects, they shipped us a bundle of old navy uniforms and we took them apart and made uniforms for the kids. Our best uniforms, which we wore on Sundays for the High Mass, were the ones that were purchased brand new. They were pleated. But the other uniforms we used during the week we had to make from scratch out of the navy pants. I guess it was stuff they never used. Or maybe it was from dead soldiers. God knows. We used to joke about using dead soldiers' uniforms. They'd bring it by the bundles.

I couldn't get the hang of knitting diamond-stitch socks for the priests, so one kind nun, Sister Genevieve, taught me to crochet with a fine linen thread for making trims using my right hand. It's funny she couldn't teach me to use my left hand because she was right-handed. So I learned how to crochet right-handed and I can only crochet with my right hand.

🕮

Later on, they had marching bands in my school. I was never in the bands. This happened after I left school. Slug and Spic were in the band. The St. Joseph's all-girls pipe band was famous. They travelled across Canada, all the way to Toronto. They had a boys' band at first, then they made a girls' band.

I'm not sure what the big deal was back east. A big Canadian celebration. The St. Joseph's band was the only all-girls pipe band in the country. That's why they invited them to Toronto. They all played instruments. Slug played the drums. Some played the flutes.

🕮

The spooky attic at the mission was my biggest fear. It felt like evil lived in there. It was dark, and that's where our extra special uniforms we wore for Easter and Christmas were kept in closets. The lighting was real poor, with only one light bulb and one little window in the centre of the room. Sometimes there were bats flying around. It just sent chills up your spine. There were spooks there for real. You could feel it.

I never liked going up there alone. I was sure the devil was going to pounce out at me. I was told I was bad because I talked all the time. And I was always punished. Being punished meant you were bad. I was always talking because when I thought of something, I had to tell somebody right away.

11

My Second Year at St. Joseph's Mission

For my second year at St. Joseph's Mission, my dad brought us there from Esket by horse and wagon. It was early September 1943 when we headed out from Esket. We didn't know it but our mom must have been in labour. Soon after we got to my great-aunt Julianna's place at Sugarcane (T'exelc First Nation), Mom gave birth to Spic.

My dad's aunt Julianna was from Skeetchestn and married into Sugarcane. We always called her Schwoolianne. We usually camped overnight at her place when we came from Alkali, and we'd always have a visit with her.

When Spic was born, Julianna said, "Give that baby my name." So my parents called her Julia and gave her the second name Victorine, after our oldest sister, Victorine, who had passed away a year or two earlier. The first Victorine was only ten years old when she died, and she never went to school. So Spic's name is Julia Victorine, and she was born on September 12, 1943. I'll always remember that day. She was kind of sickly when she was little. But later she got strong.

After Spic was born, my dad brought us the rest of the way to the mission. It was only a few miles up the road from Sugarcane, but it could have been on another planet. Martha was going into grade 2, Willard was entering grade 3, and they kept me in grade 1 because I had missed so much school the year before. Life at the mission hadn't changed much. You still done a lot of praying and not too much learning. And we were still separated from our brothers and only saw them at church time when they came up to our chapel for High Mass on Sundays. We'd wave to each other as they went by. But that's as close as we got. They didn't mix us and kept us separate. So just looking across the chapel or waving was all we saw of our brothers. Yes, they had crazy ideas.

But that's the way it was. We had no choice. We were run by the Indian agent and the government. Bill Christie was the Indian agent. He was Mr. Christie. So you had to do what he said. You had to go by the rules.

≥

Our first job back at school in the fall was bringing in the potato harvest. The mission had huge root cellars. They'd bring in a truckload of apples from the

Okanagan and just unload it in the root cellar. Extra apples that couldn't fit in there were kept in boxes in the basement of the school, below the kitchen. We ate those apples first.

So we helped with the potato harvest. First they'd plow the potatoes out of the ground, then the girls had to pile them here and there on the field to let them air out and dry for a few days. Then we'd bag them up in sacks and pile the sacks in bunches, then the wagon would take them to the root cellar.

There were milk cows as well as beef cows at the mission. The boys done all the cow milking, then they'd separate the milk. But we never had the cream. We weren't lucky to get any butter either. But the priests and nuns did. We done the work and they got the goodies.

Cecilia as a student at St. Joseph's Mission.

Old Brother Collins who chased you when you brought him shoes to repair also looked after the garden all summer. He was so proud of his garden. They had big potato gardens out toward the Three Mile, on the other side of the mission going out. They also had a huge vegetable garden right in the centre of the mission before it became a playground. So old Brother Collins had his carrots and beans and, God knows, tomatoes. Everything.

🖋

They weren't training you to be a lawyer or a doctor at the mission. I always wanted to be a teacher or a lawyer or a journalist. Well, now that I'm teaching the Secwepemctsín language and culture, I guess I sort of became a teacher. A language teacher. That's as close to my wishes as I got.

I had to learn to read and write Secwepemctsín after I got out of the mission, because they certainly didn't teach it there. I'm still learning.

At the mission we weren't even allowed to speak our language. You'd get punished if they caught you speaking Secwepemctsín, Tŝilhqot'in or Dakelh. It was their law, so we had to kind of sneak around it. When we first got to the mission, we had to learn to speak English because we only spoke Secwepemctsín at home. Then we had to learn to read and write English.

Some of the girls, when they left school, said they forgot their language. I don't know how anybody could forget a language once they know it. I give my dad a lot of credit for that. He always told us to be proud of what we were. He said, "Don't look down on your people. Never, ever look down. Never,

ever think you're better because you went to school." Some of our people who went to school and on to high school were a little snobbier toward their own people. My dad made sure we didn't do that. He was a good dad.

The Kids from Nazko

Nellie George was the first student to come from Nazko. This was probably two years after I started at the mission. She had to have been thirteen when she got there. Her dad Zalloway George brought her and dropped her off.

Nellie was such a lonely person when she was just there by herself. But the next year Zalloway brought a whole bunch more Nazko kids, including Nellie's younger sister Sophie. The Nazkos were just coming in. Zalloway was forward thinking in that he wanted his kids to have an education. Since Nellie was older, she only went up to grade 2 before she had to leave. Sophie was quite a bit younger than Nellie.

Some of the Nazko kids who came with Sophie were older too. Some of the boys were almost six feet tall and were only there for a year or two because the mission only took you until you were sixteen years old.

Special Visitors

My parents stopped in to visit us at the mission two or three times a year. They'd come a couple of times before Christmas, like on their way up to the meadow where my dad guided his hunters. Then they'd swing by again on their way to Alkali for Christmas. Then at Easter time they'd come again.

We'd always be so excited when our parents came to visit. We'd be happy for a couple of days anyway. They would come by to see us because we weren't allowed to go anywhere for ten months straight. They weren't very long visits. They stayed in the visitors' cabin and could put their horses in the barn overnight.

But we were still separated. My sisters and I couldn't visit our parents with our brothers. They didn't let us visit together as a family. Then the rules started to relax a bit. During my last two years at school, they started letting us go home at Christmas and Easter. Two weeks for Christmas and a week at Easter.

ঽ

I remember when World War II was over and returning soldiers Garnet Squinahan and Adolph Johnson from Esk'et came to the mission. The nun called all the Alkalis to come to the parlour because the soldiers wanted to visit with all the Esk'etemc kids. When we got to the parlour, we were all shy and stood in the corner. We didn't know what to say.

They came with Jimmy Wycotte, a returning soldier from Sugarcane. Jimmy came to visit his daughter Kathy Wycotte, who was in school with us. So Garnet and Adolph came with him, and they called all the Alkalis to come to the parlour. But we didn't really know them because we were kids and we'd never communicated with them before. They were kind of strangers to us. We'd seen Garnet around. Our family would stop and camp at their meadow, on our way to Moose Meadow once in a while, because they were partway between Esk'et and Lac la Hache. So we knew the Squinahans a little bit. But after we went to school we never saw them again.

Even some of the kids from Esk'et were complete strangers to us. They were from Alkali but we'd never communicated with them or hung out. So we didn't know them. When you're seven or eight and live on an isolated meadow most of the time and go to the mission for the first time, you don't know most of the people from home. But we got to know them once we got to the mission. The Alkali bunch were the biggest bunch at the mission.

We made friends with kids from Dog Creek and Canim Lake because we had family there. The Sugarcanes and Soda Creek kids kind of stuck together because they were more related to each other. Two reserves close by each other.

12

Sister John the Baptist

Things changed a lot after Sister John the Baptist became principal of the school. This was during my last two years at the mission, after that mean Sister Superior Josephine had left. I never saw her smile once.

Sister John the Baptist was my mom's age. When my mom was in her last year of school and during the two years she worked at the mission before she married my dad, she and Sister John the Baptist did stuff together. They used to sleigh ride together. Sister John the Baptist was just a young nun then.

So once she became the new principal, things started to change. We'd have picnics and other activities with the boys and girls mixing together. There'd be dances and skating parties we could do together. And to top it off, they gave us hot cocoa and buns or whatever treats they had for us.

Life got a lot more tolerable once Sister John the Baptist became the school principal at St. Joseph's Mission. Boys and girls were allowed to mix and have social outings together. I was a member of the girls softball team. I am at the front on the left holding the baseball bat.

Alkali had a rodeo on May 24, and for my last couple of years at the mission they took us all to the Alkali rodeo. The girls rode in one cattle truck and the boys in another. And away we went. That was fun. Most of us stood all the way from the mission to Alkali in the back of the cattle trucks.

This was a big change. Before that, we never mixed at all. The only times the boys and girls saw each other was in the classroom if we happened to be in the same grade, or in the chapel. The classrooms were mixed but separated, with the boys on one side of the room and the girls on the other. The same with the chapel. The boys were on the right and the girls were on the left, and we weren't allowed to talk to each other.

But once Sister John the Baptist took over as principal, we had dancing parties and picnics with the boys and girls together, and we mixed in the classroom, and we were allowed to talk to one another.

13

Summer Respite
Back Home with Family

For the nine years I spent going to school at the mission, I always looked forward to the two months I got to spend at home with my family during the summer. When school was over at the end of June, our parents would be right there to pick us up. The first thing we did was take in the Williams Lake Stampede because it happened right about that time.

Each family had their own special camping spots along the hill above the rodeo grounds where the grandstands are today. It was the Sugarcanes, Alkalis, Canim Lake and then the Tŝilhqot'ins on the right-hand side. And it was tents all around. And they'd all get their wine bottles and sit around and have a big party. And all the school kids would visit back and forth.

⚜

My dad always had racehorses. He and Pierro Squinahan and Alfred Sandy all had racehorses. They bought them from Scotty Frizzi after I started school. After racing them at the Williams Lake Stampede, they'd head up to Quesnel and race their horses up there. Horse racing was my dad's passion and entertainment. He loved doing racehorses.

He also had a special horse for running the mountain race at the Williams Lake Stampede. He never rode the mountain race himself but let others ride his horse for him. The mountain race started way up the mountain, high above the stampede grounds, and they'd race down the steep slope right into the rodeo grounds. Of course, once they put in the new highway to Quesnel, they had to cancel the mountain race.

Pierro, my dad's brother-in-law, usually rode Dad's mountain horse. Dad had the horse but Pierro would run the mountain race. That mountain racetrack went straight down, and our dad didn't want to risk his life. Over the years several people died or got seriously injured doing that competition. Like Dave Twan, our close family friend.

Once in a while our dad's older brother Harry would run the mountain race on his horse. But after Harry married that lady from Canoe Creek, they went down to the States to pick apples and never came back. But Dad ran the flat race. Both in Williams Lake and in Quesnel. He also rode the flat races at Esk'et.

Horse racing was my dad's passion and enjoyment.

🦌

Once the Williams Lake Stampede was over, Martha, Richard and Willard would ride Dad's racehorses to Quesnel. They never let me ride a racehorse. I wasn't serious enough. Kind of goofy. Martha was serious and Willard was serious, so I just rode one of the regular horses. We had lots of riding horses we had to keep tame for the hunters.

Since we didn't have a car, we took the team and wagon to Quesnel. It took us two days to get there. On the way up we'd usually camp at Macalister where the road runs close to the river. Coming back, we'd camp at Xatśūll Village at Soda Creek, where Mom's friend Addie Sellars lived. They had gone to school together. Addie was Felix Bob's sister.

In Quesnel they'd race their horses and we'd camp across the river from town. They had a pasture for the horses there and we paid so much per horse to feed them overnight. Then we'd all come home and it would be time to hay. Right around the time we got out of school, the fish would be coming up the Fraser River, so my mom would dry salmon while we got ready for haying.

We weren't allowed to take any dried fish or dried meat to the mission when we went back to school in September. But when our parents stopped by to visit us, they'd bring us dried meat and fish. That was our treat, our candy, and we'd sneak it into our cupboards. We all had cupboards to keep our stuff in at the mission. Martha and I would share a cupboard. Sometimes three or four of us would share a cupboard.

So we had pretty full summers helping with the haying, drying fish, watering the garden, berry picking and hide tanning.

One year it was a wet summer and we were still up at the meadow haying when it was time for the hunters to start coming. We didn't make it back to school until the end of October, and the Indian agent, Mr. Christie, sent a rider up there to tell my dad to get us back to school or he was going to get the cops after us. Mr. Christie wasn't too scary, though once in a while he'd try a bluff. But we were happy to be missing school.

14

Racism in Williams Lake and Within Esk'et

When I was growing up, Indigenous people weren't allowed in the cafés or hotels in Williams Lake. Sin Tooie's was the only restaurant we could go into because it was Chinese. He was on First Avenue just down the street from the Elks Hall, but we weren't allowed in the other cafés. The Bank of Commerce was right there, and the ladies' wear next door. Sin Tooie's was right across the street from them. But there's nothing there now.

Sin Tooie's Story

—Sage Birchwater

Irene Stangoe tells the story of Sin Tooie coming to Canada from China in 1910 in her book *History and Happenings in the Cariboo-Chilcotin: Pioneer Memories*. He was only twenty years old, and it took him seventeen days to make his way from Ashcroft to Alexis Creek, where he went to work for Alex Graham's C-1 Ranch.

In a 1966 interview, he told Stangoe he worked for various ranches doing "any damn thing" from cowboying to cooking to mending farm machinery to butchering animals to irrigating. Stangoe describes him as BC's "only Chinese cowboy."

Then after thirty years he gave up the rough life and moved to Williams Lake to become a cook at the Royal Café in the Lakeview Hotel. In 1947 he opened his own Williams Lake café on First Avenue, and later he added a rooming house.

"I start it for the Indians so they have somewhere to go," he told Stangoe.

Irene Stangoe, *History and Happenings in the Cariboo-Chilcotin: Pioneer Memories* (Heritage House, 2000), 57–58.

Mackenzie's Store is on the right-hand side looking up Oliver Street just past the Ranch Hotel. The Famous Café is across the street on the left.

In Williams Lake, if you went into town, Indigenous people had to clear the streets by 9:00 p.m. or even earlier, by six o'clock, because you had to be off the streets because the stores would close.

After our parents picked us up from school, and once the rodeos and the horse races were over, my family would shop at Mackenzie's Store in Williams Lake to get the supplies we needed. Flour, sugar and rice we'd get by the hundred-pound sack because it had to last us all summer until fall. Alkali Store was too expensive to buy the bulk supplies, and they didn't have the hundred-pound stuff anyway. Then, when they brought us back to the mission at the end of the summer, they'd load up again for winter before heading home.

We could go into Mackenzie's to buy groceries, but Native women weren't encouraged to go into the ladies' wear store. We got most of our stuff like that by mail orders through Eaton's or Simpson-Sears catalogues. They'd watch every move you made when you went into the store.

The Famous Café Ice Cream Caper

One year, when I was eight or nine years old, we were ready to head home after our parents had picked us up from the mission and we had taken in the Stampede and horse racing and finished shopping at Mackenzie's Store. It was a hot day and our mom told us she'd get each of us an ice cream cone at the Famous

Jessie Foster worked in the provincial courthouse just up the street from Mackenzie's Store and the Famous Café.

Café across the street from Mackenzie's Store. "Just wait out here and I'll go in and get it," she told us.

When our mom walked in the door to order the ice cream, this woman started complaining. "What's that dirty Indian doing in our café?"

The woman was Jessie Foster, a government employee who worked at the courthouse just up the street. My mom gave her a dirty look but didn't say anything. When she brought us our ice cream cones, she told us to eat them slowly. "I'm going to wait for that lady to come out and I'll beat the shit out of her."

My mom was tough. She took men on. If anybody said anything off with her, even if it was a man, she'd face up to him too. She'd punch him out.

Just for an ice cream cone, my mom had to almost get in a fight. If Jessie Foster had come out of the café that time, my mom would have beat her up. Jessie Foster probably knew that, so she stayed inside. She outwaited my mom.

Years later, after Lenny and I were married, Jessie Foster came to Alkali Lake Ranch to run the store. She must have been retired from the government by that time. She was a long-time friend of the Riedemanns. She used to come out to the ranch and stay over on weekends. When I was working for the Riedemanns in 1951 and '52, I'd see her there. They'd invite her out as a guest.

The courthouse flag pole is on the left in front of the Canadian Imperial Bank of Commerce. Mackenzie's Store is on the other side of the bank. Across the street is the Famous Café.

Alkali Store was the only place close to the village where people in Esk'et could pick up the little things they needed. And I don't know if my mom ever spoke to Jessie Foster about the rude comments she had made many years earlier at the Famous Café in Williams Lake. Jessie probably forgot all about what she had said to her.

Our mom might have mumbled something to her though. She probably would have. I can imagine her asking Jessie what she was doing out in our country after calling us down in her country.

My mom didn't take guff from nobody. She had to fight her way all the way up, dealing with prejudice from both the Natives and the whites. She was Indian as far as the white people were concerned, and she was white from the First Nations' point of view. So she was kind of a nobody stuck in the middle.

Jessie Foster wasn't particularly sociable when she came out to run the store. She was never friendly and never said to come to the house and have tea or anything like that. When Mrs. Lipscomb ran the store when I was a little girl, she'd invite us over for tea. I never knew much about the Lipscombs or where they came from, but she was really nice. They never came to the reserve, though. The Riedemanns didn't allow their workers to go up to the reserve.

Prejudice Within the Esk'etemc Community

They called my mom séme7 at Esk'et. That's the Secwepemctsín word for a white person or somebody of European ancestry. They called her that just to bug her because her biological father was white. And they called us kids sésme7, or "little white people."

My dad was so successful with his hunting outfit, I wonder if they weren't just jealous of my mom. Of course she was the best moccasin maker and hide tanner in the village. You could sew the buckskin she made with just a regular needle, it was that soft. She was so fussy tanning her hides. You had to do it right.

It kind of bugged us kids to have people call us sésme7. We always made sure we had a pocket full of rocks and our slingshots handy when we hit the reserve. We'd go on the warpath with those other little Indians that called us sésme7. And Richard had his own way of getting even. He'd say, "Okay, we'll go steal their eggs at night." So we'd all go with Richard and he'd crawl through that little hole to get into the chicken coop, and he'd gather all the eggs and pass them out to us. We'd steal all their eggs. We had to get even somehow.

Yes, we had to fight the battles. My mom had to as well. But we had friends on the reserve too. And we had friends from all over. And then we got to know our relations in Canoe Creek, Canim Lake, Dog Creek, Sugarcane and Soda Creek.

🍃

We spent so much time at Moose Meadow that we hardly knew some of the other kids from Esk'et. When we went to school, people would say, "This person's from Alkali." But because we never associated with that bunch on the other side of the church, we didn't know them.

Even on the reserve there was prejudice. They were the upper crust and their family wouldn't let their kids associate with the "wild Indians."

The kids from other Secwépemc communities closer to town, who had more to do with white people than we did, called the kids from Esk'et "stick Indians." We didn't interact with white people like they did. The only white person we saw around Esk'et was the storekeeper.

We would only come to Esk'et to plant our potatoes and look after our vegetable garden. Then we'd go back out to the meadow again. Depending on the weather, we'd go back and forth to water and weed the garden a couple of times. Things should have got watered more probably. Everybody had to look after their own stuff. We'd harvest everything at the end of the summer and put it in the root cellar.

They had a big irrigation ditch going right across the field above the different family gardens. And when it was our turn to irrigate, we'd run the water down to our garden. People would say, "Oh, Amelia's stealing water." But they didn't dare face her. You know, they didn't say it to her face. Men and women were scared of my mom because she stood up for herself. She didn't wait for my dad to stand up for her either. She had to fight for herself ever since she was in school because she was part white. People called her séme7 and never called her Amelia. They were mean to my mom.

Squaw Hall

Squaw Hall was built in the early 1950s as a place for Indigenous people to have their dances during the Williams Lake Stampede. Indigenous people weren't allowed in the Elks Hall where the white dances were held.

Squaw Hall was an outdoor dance hall in Williams Lake they built for the First Nations people at the stampede grounds. I think it got constructed around the time I got out of the mission in 1951 when I was sixteen years old. They didn't want Indigenous people dancing in the Elks Hall during the stampede. That was for the whites. So they built Squaw Hall for us to keep us separate. We had good bands and we'd dance till daylight with Hilary Place and his band.

But then the white people started coming down from the Elks Hall once their dance had shut down for the night, and they ruined our Squaw Hall. They'd be all half-cut and wild and woolly, throwing bottles back and forth. They had to put a net over top of the dance floor because bottles were flying in and out. But the net didn't hold out too good because the rocks just got bigger. Pretty soon the dance floor would be a sea of broken glass.

That's why they had to shut it down. They got rid of Squaw Hall because it was getting too dangerous.

PART 3

Five Years Between Residential School and Marriage

15
My First Paid Job

They kicked me out of school at the mission in 1951 because I was sixteen years old. That was the age they stopped teaching you. According to the school records, I had been there nine years from September 1942 to June 1951. The Indian Residential School Quarterly Return record dated September 30, 1951, says I'd completed grade 8 in the Domestic Science Program and was "discharged—of age."

That summer of 1951, at sixteen, I was ready and raring. I spent time with my uncle Bert Johnson and his wife Adele at Forest Grove when I first left school. That's when the sawmills were starting to come in. They never had kids of their own, but Adele always babysat for my mom. They took Spic and Slug quite often, and I stayed with them for quite a while one winter. They were a good aunt and uncle, but my mom didn't want me to stay with them because they were a long ways off and she heard they drank a lot on weekends. They hardly ever drank when I was with them.

Then I got offered a job at Alkali Lake Ranch. That was my first paid job, cleaning house and waxing wooden floors for the Riedemanns. They had to be shiny and up to snuff. Celestine Rosette picked me to work with her at the ranch. The girl working with her had quit, so Celestine asked me if I'd be her helper. They paid me fifty dollars a month to clean the Big House, and other people at the ranch would hire me to clean their house or babysit once in a while.

Celestine was good to me. She was my mother's age and a real mother to me. She and my mother went to school together. She was from Esk'et and married a Rosette. She showed me everything. How to clean and how to put wax on the hardwood floors.

That's where I met Lenny DeRose, my future husband, for the first time. He was twenty-two years old and was one of the ranch hands. Celestine and I would come down to lunch at the mess hall, and that's where Lenny and I first saw each other.

That winter Mrs. Riedemann invited Celestine and me to stay in the basement of the Big House instead of walking back and forth to the reserve. We shared a bedroom downstairs. She said we could stay there for the winter because I would have needed firewood all winter at our house in the village, and it would have been cold because my parents were back at the meadow. My mom would check up on me. She'd tell me she was hearing bad stories about me. I think she wanted to keep me in line, so she'd just say that.

Lenny was a friend of Nene and Dave Twan. They kind of adopted him when he was in his early teens around Quesnel and Alexandria after he set out on his own from Wells, where he grew up.

Dave Twan was the Alkali Ranch foreman in charge of farming and hay production. His brother Bill Twan was the cattle boss. Evelyn Maurice was Dave and Bill's sister. She was actually their niece but was raised as their sister. She lived there with her husband Hermie, who was part of the ranching crew. I did

Lenny and me about ten years after we were married.

housework for Evvy and Hermie, and for Bill and Nanna Twan, but never for Nene and Dave. Nene always done her own housework. She only had one kid, Danny, at home by that time. Their older son Jackie had already left home.

My mom knew Dave Twan's mom, Rosalie Hunt Twan. Once in a while Evvy would get me to clean her house or babysit the kids when she and Hermie went to town, and that's where I met Rosalie. She told me she was Dakelh (Carrier) but I never really knew where from. Later on, Nene told me that Rosalie was from Alexandria and Quesnel. To me, Dakelh were from Nazko. I didn't know Quesnel was Dakelh. I should have put two and two together because a bunch of Nazkos came to our school when I was there.

🔖

The Riedemanns were upper crust. Mario Riedemann, Martin's dad, always had a stiff neck. Straight as a poker. But his wife Elizabeth was more like an ordinary person. She liked to sew and had a big sewing room up in the attic. She sewed most of her daughters' clothes and stuff and may have made shirts for her boys too. She liked sewing and she liked gardening. She had a big flower garden. I don't think she had a vegetable garden because they had two Chinese vegetable gardeners. But she loved flowers and had all kinds of flowers out in her backyard. She was always back there or upstairs sewing.

But Mario just walked around like he was king.

His dad, Heinrich von Riedemann, was quite different. He was really nice. He'd come up and visit maybe every six months from Vancouver. He was a really ordinary person. And he was the one with the money. He'd leave Celestine and me a twenty-dollar bill each when he'd leave. Twenty dollars in those days was like a hundred dollars today, and he'd give us each a twenty-dollar tip. We never got any tips from the other Riedemanns, but the old man always tipped us when he left. Heinrich bought the ranch for his son Mario from Charles Wynn-Johnson in 1939, just before World War II. They said they barely got out of Austria.

ᕗ

Celestine and I would play canasta in the evenings after work. We took turns going here and there to different households every night. One night we'd go to Bill and Nana Twan's, then another night to Evvy and Hermie's. Then we'd go down to Dave and Nene's. That's where I got to know Lenny better. He was always down there when we'd play canasta. Lenny never played canasta himself. But he was there a couple of times. Lenny was never a card person.

DEDE: We played cards every night after supper when we were growing up, but Dad never played cards with us. We'd do the dishes and Mom would put on the tea and we'd sit around and play cards. But Dad never played.

CECELIA: So I guess that's where Lenny and I started to go together. There were dances on the reserve and he'd come up. White guys weren't allowed up there, but he used to come anyway.

Martha and I Go Trapping

So I met Lenny when I was sixteen, then after a year and a half working for the Riedemanns with Celestine, I quit my job and Martha and I went up to Moose Meadow to see what the old folks done. This was my second winter after getting out of school, and we were curious. We had to go up and see what went on in the winter up there. We found out and never went back again. There was nothing to do.

We learned how to trap from our parents. A little bit of beaver but not too much. Mostly squirrels. They didn't want us ruining the beaver hides. But they trusted us with the squirrels. But the squirrels had lice that ran up our arms while we were skinning them. We caught a few weasels too. They were a little more money but they were quite stinky. We'd get the odd weasel but never got into the bigger stuff like marten, mink, coyote or lynx. We thought we'd get lots of money for our squirrels because Scotty Frizzi, the fur buyer, was a family friend.

We started trapping and snaring squirrels, but that wasn't fun anymore. So we decided to try shooting them. Our parents told us if we were going to start shooting them, we had to make sure we only shot them in the head. We thought we could do that, but it didn't always work out that way. A squirrel's head is very small and they move around so quick. So sometimes we'd miss and shoot them in the body, and we got a lot less money for squirrels with big holes in their skins.

My dad was a good shot, and my mom could really shoot them too. When my dad went hunting, he always came back with something. And his eyesight was way better than my mom's. But his hearing wasn't that good. My mom's hearing was better, but her eyes weren't as good as my dad's.

So Martha and I just had to be nosy and see what our parents done up there in the winter. But it wasn't that much fun. Besides trapping squirrels and hunting squirrels, we snared a few rabbits and stuff like that and took our fur to Scotty Frizzi a couple of times, before Christmas and again before Easter.

Scotty lived up the road from Alkali toward Springhouse. He got a piece of land and he made a little store. His brother Karl had a place there too. They came from the old country, from Switzerland originally, and they had quite the accents. My dad was working at the mission when Scotty and Karl showed up from Switzerland. They didn't know English, so they had to learn.

A lot of people at Esk'et didn't like Alkali Store, so they'd go up to Scotty's place to buy stuff and sell him their fur. He had more interesting stuff than what you could find in Alkali Store, but it was farther away from the village, and you'd have to ride up there on horseback or take your team and wagon or sleigh. Most people at Esk'et didn't own a car. We'd stop in there on our way back and forth to Moose Meadow, or when we travelled between Esk'et and Williams Lake.

Scotty married Josephine, who was half Tŝilhqot'in from Tl'esqox (Toosey) near Riske Creek. She looked white and must have had a white dad, but she could understand Tŝilhqot'in. Karl had a little place just across the road. Some acreage. A meadow and a hayfield. He married an Isnardy girl and they raised their family there.

Karl had two girls and a boy close in age to Willard, Martha and me. When we were kids and staying in the village, the Frizzi kids would come down and play with us. They'd ride down by horseback and play all day with us, then ride home again in the evening. So they'd come to play and their mom would send a can of jam or something because they had no playmates up where they lived. Just themselves, and they probably fought with each other.

🝣

It was quite boring just trapping, cutting wood and keeping the fire going all winter, and we got tired of snaring and shooting squirrels, so Martha and I just spent one winter up there. Going to school at the mission kind of modernized us in a way.

At the same time, that winter we helped our mom with her buckskin gloves and stuff like that. She also spun her own wool and done all her own knitting. She'd buy raw sheep fleeces from Felker's at the 134 Mile House and would hand spin it with a spindle on her knee. Then she'd knit gloves and socks and stuff. She even made a sweater for Felix. He always had a hand-knitted sweater, toque and gloves.

We helped her wash the fleeces and clean them to get all the grass and stuff out of them. Then she'd card it and spin all her own wool. That's one thing they never taught us at the mission. They never had sheep at the mission and never brought in any raw fleeces to show us how to clean and prepare wool for spinning and knitting. So our Domestic Science Program didn't teach you everything.

The only thing they taught us was to knit diamond-stitch socks for the priests. But I could never figure out how to do the diamond design.

16

Working at the Mission

During the winter we spent trapping with our folks at the meadow, we came down to Esk'et for Christmas and then for Easter. When we came down at Easter, Father Price, the missionary responsible for Esk'et, said they needed some cooks at the mission. So Martha and I decided to go over and check it out. They offered us jobs right away, so we went back to the meadow, packed up our stuff and went to work at the mission. I had just turned eighteen.

This was April 1953 and the new school had just opened. Myrtle Stager from Mount Currie also worked there with us. Our boss in the kitchen was Sister Rose Alma.

I can't remember what the wages were, but they paid you by the hour. It was more than I got at Alkali Lake Ranch. You worked a split shift from morning to 1:00 p.m., then you got 1:00 to 3:00 p.m. off, then you worked from 3:00 to 7:00 p.m. So we were in the kitchen cooking breakfast, lunch and supper for three hundred kids and staff in the new school.

Everything in the new school was modern and automatic. Big automatic dishwashers, big sinks. You just stuck the dirty plates in the dishwasher and ran them through. Then you'd stack some more in there. When I was a student in the old school, we had tubs of wash water at the end of each table. There were sixteen of us at a table and we took turns washing, rinsing and drying our own dishes. Then we'd reset the table. Two would wash, two would rinse and two would dry. But the new school was all modern. The staff ran the automatic dishwasher but the kids still had to collect the dirty dishes and bring them to be washed. Once they were clean, the kids had to count the plates and put them at the ends of the tables for the next meal and set the tables with all the knives and forks.

❧

Shortly after we started work at the mission, a big event was held to celebrate Father François Marie Thomas for his fifty years serving as a priest there in the Order of Mary Immaculate.

It was Father Thomas who married my grandparents Andre Dick Johnson and Margaret (Makrit) Seymour in 1899, and in 1902 he baptized my dad Matthew Dick and his twin brother Joe. He also baptized me in 1935.

Father Thomas was the priest for everybody in the Cariboo Chilcotin—the Secwépemc, Tŝilhqot'in and Dakelh.

🍃

The quality of food was way better in the new school than it was when I was a student. We served big pots of mush in the morning and big pots of soup at lunch. For supper we baked big macaroni casseroles in the oven. And the students got butter then. They had this little thing of butter and you could butter your own bread. They still had milk cows, but they had automatic milking machines by that time. My brother Willard had to milk by hand when he went to school, and the boys had to separate the cream by hand. But when I was working in the kitchen, they might have bought milk from the store by then.

Of course, we had to go by standards because it was government, and they had to go by union rules in the kitchen. They had a walk-in freezer and a walk-in fridge, and the new school had big propane stoves. In the old school, all they had were wood-burning cookstoves that took big long wood. They were already building the new school when I left there in 1951. The new school had the boys and girls, priests and nuns all in the same building. The girls and the nuns were at one end and the boys and the priests were at the other end.

When Martha and I worked there, our sister Irene was still in school, and so were Spic and Slug and our little brother Felix.

17

Our Lady of the Cape Shrine Pilgrimage

Martha and I had been working at the mission for a year when we heard about this big religious event happening in Quebec in the summer of 1954. There's a shrine in Trois-Rivières, about halfway between Montreal and Quebec City, where some people said the Virgin Mary appeared to these two children or something. Some kind of Catholic faith miracle happened there and it's called Our Lady of the Cape Shrine. It was the hundredth anniversary since the statue of Our Lady of the Cape Shrine had been venerated back in 1854, so they wanted as many Indigenous people back there as possible. So I went on the train with my girlfriend Joan Beliveau. This would have probably been in July, once the kids had gone home from school for the summer. I was nineteen years old by then.

My sister Martha originally applied to go on the pilgrimage and was accepted, but then she chickened out and decided not to go. So Joan went in her place. She borrowed Martha's buckskin coat my mom had made, borrowed Martha's ID and acted as my sister. But she was white. I mean she was dark French, but you could tell she wasn't Indigenous. Anyway she went in Martha's place, and away we went on the train. She travelled as First Nations all the way. Her grandfather was French from back there.

Joan was the grade 2 teacher at St. Joseph's Mission residential school when I met her, and she taught me and Martha all these things about being white. She was the same age as Martha and me, and she showed us a lot of the ropes about how to function in white society.

When I was a kid growing up, Indigenous people didn't go anywhere by themselves. They didn't go into stores, didn't do this and didn't do that. But when Joan came, she'd say, "Let's go to town and go shopping."

We normally didn't just go to town to go shopping. Like if my mom took us into town, she'd take us into the ladies' wear and we'd pick out what we needed. We didn't call it shopping. We just went and bought the necessities.

And then restaurants, we didn't dare go into a restaurant just to go into a restaurant. We didn't even go into a restaurant. White people went into restaurants. But Joan taught us how to do that. After a movie she'd say, "Let's go down to the Chinese restaurant to meet." After the movie we'd all go there. So we did more than just go to a movie.

She was the first "white" teacher at the mission besides the nuns. Nuns are white, but they're all black actually. Joan was the first ordinary person to teach there. The first secular teacher who didn't represent the church.

With Joan we learned what ordinary people do. Go to a movie, go for a walk, go to the restaurant; fool around, chase boys, just act ordinary; just be a regular girl. Joan taught us that we were equal as Indigenous people. Because Williams Lake was one of the worst towns for being prejudiced.

❧

We went as far as Winnipeg on the train, then by bus from Winnipeg to Quebec to get to this shrine. In my teenage mind I was just going for the ride. It was nothing about religion as far as I was concerned.

Joan had an aunt living nearby, so during a break in the action we left the gang and went and visited her. But her aunt spoke only French, so Joan and her aunt had a hard time understanding each other. Then we continued on to Quebec City. They had tents all over, and Joan and I had a tent together. There were cops or whatever guarding the tents and we got chummy with them, so they took us out on the town one night.

We weren't allowed in taverns, but they took us to a tavern that served supper. I didn't drink then, but it was a tavern where you could drink. I was never a drinker. I was more like my mother that way. Booze was never my thing.

Anyway they took us out on the town, took us for dinner and brought us back to our tent. And they spoke only French. It was quite the experience. Dating somebody who spoke only French was quite interesting.

On our way home we stopped in Ottawa and they had a big celebration at the Parliament Buildings. I got picked to shake hands with Prime Minister Louis St. Laurent. I have a picture of him and me shaking hands. I was wearing my buckskin jacket and I think that's why they picked me. Joan was wearing Martha's jacket but she was white. So they picked me out of the crowd for the picture with the prime minister.

My mom had made Martha and me a buckskin jacket each. Then, later on, she made us give them to our younger sisters. I had to give mine to Slug and she made Martha give hers to Spic. Spic still has hers but Slug went and gave mine away. I never should have given it to her. I should have known her better. But I had to do what my mother said. I don't know why Mom made us give them our jackets. She probably wanted the jackets to stay in the family. Or maybe by that time she wasn't making buckskin jackets any longer. They were probably the last ones she made.

They picked me to shake hands with Prime Minister Louis St. Laurent because I was wearing my buckskin jacket. In the background is Father Gontran Laviolette OMI, the Oblate commissioner for Indian and Eskimo Affairs.

DEDE: There's a picture of Spic and Slug wearing those jackets when they were Stampede Queens. Both Slug and Spic were Indigenous Stampede Queens.

CECELIA: We came back on the train and got off in Calgary and took in the Calgary Stampede. Joan had an aunt living south of Calgary. I don't know which town. But we'd hitchhike into the Calgary Stampede every day and hitchhike home every night. That was the only time I ever got to the Calgary Stampede. I never did go back. Anyway that was our experience.

LULU: We took Mom to Jasper because we had friends there who had a hotel. We were visiting with a guy and Mom said, "I was here in 1954." And he said, "You were here before the road then; you had to have come on the train at that time." And she said, "Yeah, we came by train."

A Story I Never Told Before

CECELIA: One experience I never told anyone the whole story about happened after I got back from the Our Lady of the Cape Shrine pilgrimage in Quebec.

I heard they were renovating the church at Esk'et, and the Secwépemc missionary priest, Father Price, was overseeing the renovations. My day off from working in the kitchen at the mission was Thursday, and that's the day Father Price started going out there. He started inviting me to go with him to Esk'et and I jumped at the chance. I got to visit my family while he was inspecting the work on the church.

Then after the third or fourth time, he decided to take a shortcut home to the mission through Springhouse and ran into a huge mud hole. He said he was worried he might not make it through the mud hole, but it might have just been an excuse to stop. There we were in the middle of nowhere. I told him we should turn around and go back, and that's when he tried to get fresh with me. So I just got out of the car and I was going to run for the bush. We weren't too far from Esk'et and I knew I could walk back there.

Then Father Price apologized and said he acted out of line and said we could say the rosary all the way back to the mission. He happened to have a rosary wrapped around his steering wheel. So I got back in and he drove us back without any further incident, saying the rosary all the way.

Needless to say, I never went out to Alkali with him again after that. And I never told a soul about it until a second incident happened a while later.

I was all by myself in our shared room, which was the old infirmary on the fourth floor, next to the priests' and brothers' side. The priests could enter from their side, but the door was locked on our side so we couldn't go through into their quarters. I didn't know where the girls had gone for the night. I later found out they went to a movie.

I woke in the night startled. There was a man standing by my bed and I hadn't heard him come in. Then he spoke and said not to be frightened. It was Father Price. Then he asked if it would be okay if he could lie beside me for a while.

I was so frightened I could hardly breathe and I could hear my heart pounding. He said he just wanted to wake me. I just held on to my blankets and prayed he'd leave. It seemed like forever, then he finally did go away.

The next day when Martha and Myrtle came back, I told them about it and they both gave me their own stories. Martha said the same priest was standing by her bed one night while I was away back east on the Our Lady of the Cape Shrine pilgrimage. And while we were whispering away in our room, Sister Jean, a young nun, came by. She always stopped to join us in our giggles. So we told her about what happened, and she told us to report it to Father O'Shea, the principal. So we did. Maybe a month later, Father Price was transferred to Hope. But I always felt bad or guilty about it.

He probably found out Thursday was my day off, so he decided to go out to Esk'et on Thursdays. For me it was a good opportunity to see family. I never thought he might have other things in mind, because you're innocent and he was a priest. I never thought a priest would do that.

Joan and I remained friends for the rest of our lives. The photo was taken in 2012. Courtesy Fay Buchanan

I think Joan had left her teaching job at the mission before this incident with Father Price happened, but we remained lifelong friends. We wrote letters back and forth and she'd come up and visit, and we'd go down and see her. She married a really nice guy and they had seven kids. Her married name was Joan Murphy.

DEDE: We all met Joan Beliveau Murphy. She and Mom stayed in touch. She was so friendly and so fun. She and her husband divorced and her husband remarried, and his next wife became Mom's friend too. When Joan got dementia, her kids phoned Mom and told her.

18

Lenny and I Become a Couple

When I worked at the mission, I'd always bump into Lenny here and there, sometimes at the Stampede or at different dances. They usually had a big dance for Klondike Night in the fall when everybody brought their cattle in and sold them. And during the fall fair at the end of summer, they'd have dances at the Elks Hall too. At first they didn't allow Indigenous people in the Elks Hall, but after a while they had no choice. They had to let us in. So Lenny and I would meet there at the dances.

In the spring of 1956, I quit working at the mission and went to work at Dog Creek Store for Hilary and Rita Place. I done a little bit of everything for them, housekeeping, babysitting and working in the store. That's when their "afterthought" baby, Carmen, had come along. He was a lot younger than their first two boys, Adrian and Martin. They thought they might get a girl but they got another boy. They didn't try again.

When I got there Adrian was thirteen, Martin was nine and Carmen was just a newborn. So I'd babysit him when Hilary and Rita had to go somewhere. I worked in the store mostly on weekends. Friday night was a busy night. I'd help in the store then, and sometimes during the week they'd send me down there if they wanted to do something together.

They used to have dances down at Dog Creek, and Lenny was back working for the Riedemanns at Alkali Lake by that time and he would come down. So I guess that's where we started going together. I remember the musician Taller O'Shea would come with his band every summer. They were from Vancouver and would go to different reserves.

Hilary and his kids were really good musicians too. They'd play their instruments almost every night when I was working there. Fiddle, guitar, accordion. They were all musical.

Hilary's wife Rita was First Nations. She was a Hamilton. Half Native. She was dark and looked all Indigenous. She was beautiful and was one of the first Williams Lake Stampede Queens. Her brother Buster Hamilton was our family friend who helped my dad get his own guide outfitting business. The Hamiltons were good people. They never snubbed Indigenous people like many of the other half-breeds did. And Rita and Hilary were really good to me when I was there. And they were really good together.

Lenny and me in front of St. Theresa Church in Esk'et with Lenny's best man Tommy Desmond.

DEDE: Mom saw one of the older Place boys—I think it was Martin—at the recent water settlement celebration at Esk'et. They are now Esk'et band members, and he introduced Mom to his family and told them what a wonderful person she was to them when they were little. Also, I saw Carmen Place at the University of British Columbia when I went there. He was in the law program. They are a super nice family and have remained lifelong friends.

CECELIA: I can't remember why I left working at the mission and headed to Dog Creek. I think I just quit and left. I wanted a change or whatever. Martha stayed for a while longer, but I wanted a new experience. I worked at Dog Creek all summer and in the fall I went home to Esk'et. On December 1, 1956, Lenny and I got married at St. Theresa Church in the village.

PART 4

Married Life with Lenny DeRose

19

Early Years with Lenny

I was an old maid when Lenny and I got married. Most girls got married at eighteen, between sixteen and eighteen years old, but I was twenty-one, nearly twenty-two, and Lenny had just turned twenty-eight.

Father Leo, the "Indian" priest who came to the reserve, couldn't marry us because Lenny was white. So the white priest, Father Joseph Anthony Boyle, had to marry us, even though I was Indigenous and it was at Esk'et. It was the rules and regulations.

Father Boyle never said Mass at St. Theresa Church in Esk'et, but he would come out and say Mass for the Riedemanns at Alkali Lake Ranch. My sister Martha was my maid of honour and Tommy Desmond was Lenny's best man.

Nene and Dave Twan were there, and so were all the ranch group from Alkali Lake Ranch, along with all the people from Esk'et. We had our reception at the Moore Ranch, which was part of Alkali Ranch three miles farther down the road toward Dog Creek from the village and the main

The wedding party in front of St. Theresa Church in Es'ket Village. Lenny and me with my maid of honour Martha Dick Sure and Lenny's best man Tommy Desmond.

ranch headquarters. That's where the Riedemanns said we could live after Lenny told them we were going to get married. They said we could live at the Moore Ranch and feed a herd of cows there all winter and calve them out in the spring. So that's what we done.

There was no snow on the ground on the day of our wedding, but it started snowing that evening and it snowed all night. By morning the snow had piled right up to eleven inches.

About Lenny's Parents

—Sage Birchwater

Lenny's dad Joseph DeRose was an Italian immigrant who came to Canada as a young boy with his parents. He was born in 1885 and as a young man worked on construction of the Grand Trunk Pacific Railway from McBride to Prince Rupert and on the Pacific Great Eastern Railway from Squamish to Quesnel. Upon completion of the PGE to Quesnel, Joseph DeRose moved to Prince George and married Lenny's mom, Mildred "Millie" Maude Dixon, who was born in 1904. Some say she emigrated from Wales and was living in Oxbow, Saskatchewan, when she met Joe DeRose. The couple lived in Prince George until 1934.

Joe and Millie were nineteen years apart in age, and Millie was nineteen years old when their oldest child, Roy, was born in 1923. Their daughter Patricia was born two years after that in 1925, and Lenny, the baby of the family, arrived on November 20, 1928.

Joe worked as a teamster in Prince George, then got a job at Island Mountain gold mine in Wells. When the family moved there in 1934, Lenny was still five years old. Then Joe and Millie split up and Millie took off, leaving Joe and their children to fend for themselves.

Lenny always said his mom took off to "join the wild bunch" in Vancouver. So his dad had to raise three kids on his own and keep working to feed them before Lenny had even started school. He kind of farmed the kids out to other people in the community who stepped up to help look after them.

DEDE: Dad was sitting on the step in front of his house crying because his mom was gone. She left just before he was supposed to start school. Then this dog came up. She had just given birth to a litter of puppies and she put her head on his lap. Then she went and got her puppies and moved in with him. Dad was never without a dog after that.

They used to have dogsled races in Wells, and he trained that dog to pull a sled. He used to earn money by delivering buckets of water around town. Among his customers were the "ladies of ill repute" who lived up the road between Wells and Barkerville. The dog would pull the sled up there loaded with pails of water, and the ladies would pay Dad a nickel or ten cents. So much a pail.

Dad was five when my grandma left and he was taken in by George and Anne Riviere. They probably had the biggest influence on him. He always credited them with being his real parents growing up. That's where he learned all his horsemanship. George was an incredible horseman. And Anne was too. They fed him supper and they looked after him, but didn't make him go to school. I think he still slept at Grandpa's house. He must have. But they really took him under their wing.

Their daughter Lorraine thought of Dad more like a brother. He kind of ran wild in the community until he left. But he left with a horse he had saved up to buy, hauling water. He bought that horse under George's guidance, and that's the horse he rode down to Soda Creek with two other young friends at fourteen years old.

SONNY: Our dad and Eugene Johnson left Wells together to become cowboys when they were fourteen. There were three of them that headed out together. I can't remember the third guy's name.

DEDE: George Riviere is the one who taught Dad how to break and train horses. Dad got that life skill before he left Wells and rode his horse to Soda Creek. After that he met Dave and Nene Twan, who kind of adopted him down there and were kind of like parents to him as well.

Grandpa Joe worked in the mine and he also had a restaurant, so he was always working. Dad's brother Roy went to war, and Grandpa set up Dad's sister Pat to board with a family because he didn't want her on her own. But Dad just ran wild in the community.

Dad suffered from dyslexia. When he went to school it was really hard for him because he couldn't write. He could read but he couldn't write. So he found school very challenging. Coincidentally my brother Wessey also had dyslexia and struggled in school. Both of them made up for it with their outgoing personalities. They were both really social. But both of them struggled with writing. Dad read like crazy but he couldn't write.

And Dad was a good horseman in spite of his temper. He never did beat on a horse. He had the reputation for being a good cow boss.

CECILIA: The winter we were married, Danny Twan came to live with us at the Moore Ranch. His dad Dave Twan was in the hospital in Vancouver and his mom Nene got a job in Dog Creek working for Hilary and Rita Place. So Danny needed a place to stay. He was thirteen years old and was going to school at the Riedemann Ranch three miles away.

DANNY TWAN: I always say I was Cecilia and Lenny's first child. I used to walk to school three miles there and back from the Moore Ranch. Then when I got home I had chores to do, packing wood for the heater. I was thirteen, and my dad Dave Twan was in a full body cast from his neck to his toes in the Chest Centre in Vancouver, right next to Vancouver General Hospital. He was that way for a year because he contracted TB.

CECILIA: So Danny lived with us and we fed cows at the Moore Ranch all that winter. Then in spring, once the calving was done and the cows were turned out, Lenny got a job working for Circle S Ranch in Dog Creek.

But before we left Alkali, our daughter DeDe (Deborah Anne DeRose) was born on June 4, 1957, in Williams Lake. She was the first of our six children.

DEDE: Mom wanted to have me at Esk'et, because Kyé7e (Grandmother Amelia Dick) had all her kids at home. So Mom was all prepared to have me at home too. But Dad said no. "You're going to the hospital," he told her. Mom argued she wanted to have her baby at home because Indigenous people never had their babies in the hospital. So naturally Mom didn't want to go there. But Dad made her.

Mom was in labour when they stopped by Esk'et to pick up Kyé7e. She was all ready to deliver me if Mom had me in the car. She had her rags and scissors and everything. Nobody could believe that Dad was making Mom have me in the hospital. Indigenous people never went to the hospital.

CECILIA: DeDe was a baby when we moved to the Mountain Ranch in Dog Creek, which was part of Circle S on the high benchland before you drop down the hill into Dog Creek Valley. The Mountain Ranch is right across the road from the old Dog Creek Airport that was built during World War II. It was still operating as an airport in 1957, and we made friends with the crew staffing the station. We'd always visit back and forth. They'd have parties there. Christmas parties or whatever. Airport dances and stuff, and they'd show movies once in a while. Lenny irrigated and hayed there and rode range all summer.

Then in the fall we moved down to the main Circle S Ranch headquarters in Dog Creek for the winter, and Lenny fed cows down there. It was better money at Circle S than what Lenny got working for the Riedemanns at Alkali Lake Ranch, and the people were really nice. We were already good friends with Hilary and Rita Place, and Nene Twan and Danny were there.

DEDE: Red and Dionne Allison were also working at Circle S, and so were Jimmy and Margaret Syme. So Mom and Dad already had a circle of friends there. Jim Syme was managing the ranch, so he was sort of Dad's boss.

So that's how come we DeRose kids have known the Allison boys all our lives. We've been friends with them ever since.

I was the only girl when we lived there with the Allisons and Symes, then my cousins Wayne and Pattie DeRose moved in with us after Dad's brother Roy and his wife Pat split up. So Dad and Mom took the boys for about a year, and I was the baby. I always told my cousins, the only time I got to be an only child and they ruined it. But I'm sure I missed them terribly when they left. It was nice having a couple of older brothers.

CECILIA: When DeDe was still a newborn, Lenny's brother Roy and his wife Pat split up for a while. So their two boys came and lived with us for almost a year, and their daughter stayed with Lenny's mom in Williams Lake. The oldest boy, Wayne, was just starting grade 1, and he'd walk to Dog Creek School. The younger one stayed home with me and DeDe.

Roy's wife Pat went north to Fort St. John, where her family lived, and Roy went up there after her. That's when we got the kids. They were with us for the whole school year. Then once Roy and Pat got back together, before school started again, they came and got the kids and moved up to Fort St. John for the rest of their lives. They bought a house and they both worked up there. Roy and Pat lived up there until they died.

DEDE: My cousin Pat(tie) sadly died when he was a young man, I think in some kind of a boating accident. My dad was devastated. They lived with us for about a year until Sonny was born. Mom was heartbroken when their parents came and got them.

CECILIA: A year after we had DeDe, our second child, Leonard Richard "Sonny" DeRose, was born on July 4, 1958, in Williams Lake. The following year, the twins David Joseph DeRose and Dennis Matthew DeRose came along. They were born in Williams Lake on June 27, 1959.

DEDE: David's and Denny's middle names are Joseph and Matthew, after Mom's dad Matthew Dick and his twin brother Joe Dick.

CECILIA: We didn't know what to name them. We were at Stampede in Williams Lake and my uncle Joe was standing there and he says, "Well what's wrong with Matthew and Joe?"

All the boys growing up at Dog Creek used to come and visit DeDe when we lived at Circle S because she was the only girl.

The Spencer family owned the Circle S Ranch when we moved there in 1957. Barbara Spencer was the family member mostly involved with the ranch. She lived at Pritchard, east of Kamloops, and Lenny worked for her there in 1954 or '55 before he headed back to Alkali Lake Ranch to work for the Riedemanns again.

At one time Circle S was called the Diamond S Ranch before the Spencer family bought it in 1942. My dad Matthew Dick used to contract hay for Diamond S before I was born. The twins David and Denny were born a few months before the Spencer family sold the Circle S in September 1959. So things were starting to change around there.

The History of Diamond S/Circle S Ranch

—Sage Birchwater

Diamond S Ranch was started by Richard Hoey in the mid-1800s. Then in 1866 he sold it to Robert Carson, who developed it into one of the largest holdings in British Columbia at that time. It took in the broad benchlands west and east of the Fraser River around Pavilion.

The Diamond S became known as Carson's Kingdom and stayed in the Carson family until it was bought by Colonel Victor Spencer in 1942.

Born in Victoria in 1882, Colonel Spencer served in the South African War, then later in World War I. In 1920 he bought the Earlscourt Ranch near Lytton, which was the first of a string of ranches he acquired. His holdings included the Pavilion Ranch, the Bryson Ranch and the Diamond S Ranch.

Diamond S Ranch was officially renamed Circle S Ranch in 1950, after Colonel Spencer acquired the Douglas Lake Ranch near Merritt.

In September 1959 the Spencer family sold the 330,000-acre Circle S Ranch to a group of Arizona ranchers, and sold the Douglas Lake Ranch to Charles "Chunky" Woodward and partners in Vancouver. Colonel Spencer died in 1960 at the age of seventy-seven.

In 1972 Lyle and Mary James, ranchers from Montana, purchased the Circle S Ranch, and they ran it for forty years. In 2012 they sold it to Douglas Lake Cattle Company, owners of Alkali Lake Ranch and Gang Ranch.

Find a Grave, https://www.findagrave.com/;

Newspapers.com, https://www.newspapers.com/;

Williams Lake Tribune archives.

20

The Divide Between Indigenous and White

My Secwépemc family and friends didn't like it when Lenny and I first got together. Indigenous people didn't like Natives marrying whites, and the whites didn't like whites marrying Indigenous people. Either way.

For one thing, all the workers and hired men at Alkali Lake Ranch weren't allowed up on the reserve. And Esk'etemc girls weren't allowed to date white guys working on the ranch.

I met Lenny, of course, because I was working on the ranch for the Riedemanns right after I got out of school. We'd come down to the bunkhouse for lunch, and that's where I met him, in the mess hall. And we saw the other workers, but we never really socialized with the men.

My mom didn't really like me marrying a white man either. But my dad was easygoing about it. He said we should marry whoever we wanted to.

My mom was always yapping about how the priests got them together and picked them to marry each other. She talked about it all her life. My dad said, "Let them pick who they want to marry," because he got tired of listening to my mom talk about that for all those years.

Anyway we just got married. Just settled in together. And later on, everybody got used to it. Because they knew Lenny and they knew me, and it wasn't a big deal.

A lot of Indigenous people when they married whites would snub other Natives. I wasn't that type. I was still me as a person. I didn't snub anybody because I was married to white.

I think that's why people from my community didn't like our people marrying whites, because they'd get "high-toned" with the other Natives.

My family was still my family and my friends were still my friends.

In the end both my dad and mom were okay with me marrying Lenny. But my dad made sure I never forgot about my Indigenous heritage. I fully intended to teach my kids Secwepemctsín, but somehow we never got around to it.

DEDE: Dad always supported Mom keeping her friends and family. And he also really encouraged Mom to teach us to speak our language. He said, "You teach them," but she said she wanted to teach us English first, because she didn't want us kids to have the same problem going to school that she did.

Because of that we didn't learn our language. But we knew it was valuable because Dad valued it. Plus if Mom taught us our language, when she got with her sisters we would know what they were talking about. But then we started figuring out what words meant and could kind of tell what they were saying.

Around the time Mom and Dad got married, Dad's mother Millie moved back to the Cariboo and bought a house in Williams Lake. She wasn't happy that Dad married an Indigenous woman. So when we would go visit in her new house in Williams Lake, us kids weren't allowed in the house because we were Native. So Mom and Dad would go in the house and have tea and we would stay outside in the yard. Mom was allowed in because she was with Dad. But Mom never went there without Dad.

So one time we went there and while we were out in the yard and Mom and Dad were inside visiting, Sonny picked all of Granny Millie's flowers. When Mom and Dad came outside, he was so happy to give Mom his flowers. Granny was so mad.

Sonny always picked wildflowers for Mom, and so did Dad. Dad would go riding and come home with big bunches of wildflowers.

21
We Move to Kamloops

Lenny had a temper, and his temper kept us on the move. Maybe it was his Italian blood, I don't know. So when things didn't go his way, he'd just up and quit and away we'd go. It seemed like we moved every six months.

DEDE: Mom had boxes all the time in case Dad quit his job and we had to move. Then we'd have to put everything we owned in boxes.

CECELIA: The twins were a year old when we left Circle S and moved to Kamloops in the summer of 1960. Lenny got a job at Heffley Creek along the North Thompson River, just north of Kamloops, riding the summer range in the mountains.

He was working for a guy named Doug, and they had another piece of the ranch up on the mountain where they ranged their cattle. So we went up there for the summer so Lenny could stir the cows around. Stir the bulls around. Sometimes the bulls would get lazy and want to sleep under a tree instead of doing their job. So we were up there staying in their range cabin all summer until a skunk drove us out.

We were all in bed sleeping one night and the dog went woof! A skunk was trying to go under the house to have a sleep and the dog woofed at him and he let out a stink. Oh my gawd, he just stunk everything in the house. We had to throw out our flour and sugar and pretty much all our food that wasn't in cans. It was horrible. And we washed our clothes several times and washed our bedding and took everything to the laundromat and used those big machines. Even after washing everything a couple of times in the laundromat, people could still smell us. The skunk smell was horrible, you could hardly breathe. And yet it wasn't a direct hit. It was outside the house. He aimed at the dog but the smell came inside the house. We moved out and back to the main ranch and spent the winter there.

In the spring of 1961, a man by the name of Jose Ramon Somavia came and hired Lenny to work for him. His wife was a big millionaire from the United States, and they bought three new ranches around Kamloops. One of them was up the mountain above Savona. Somavia hired Lenny to manage the

Whispering Pines Ranch and look after the irrigation. We were just there for the summer until the hay was done.

One day our neighbours up the mountain above Savona told us they had a harness for sale. They were an older couple who had bought a tractor and had no use for the harness any longer. So they wondered if we knew anyone who might want it. It was almost like new, so I wrote my parents and asked them if they wanted another harness.

My mom wrote right back and said yes. "Tell them we're interested." She said they'd come and have a look and would probably buy it because it sounded like a good deal. So we met them down in Savona and brought them home and took them over to our neighbours' place to check out the harness.

Since my parents never did drive or own a motor vehicle, they got Mike Isnardy to drive them down. On their way through Cache Creek, they noticed a girl from Esk'et waitressing in the café. My dad was so happy to see one of our girls working in the public, so he went over and spoke to her in Secwepemctsín. But the girl spoke back in English and told him she didn't understand what he was saying.

My dad was surprised at this. Then he got upset. By the time he got to our place above Savona, he was both mad and sad, and almost crying. "Don't you ever say you don't understand if somebody speaks to you in Secwepemctsín!" he scolded me.

He caught me by surprise, because I would never do that. "Why would I do that?" I asked. "I know Secwepemctsín." I told him that's something I'd never do. Then my dad explained what happened.

This girl told my dad she didn't understand Secwepemctsín, and here she had been raised by her grandmother. She probably knew more Secwepemctsín than I did.

She was working there with Nora Twan, and I guess she heard Nora telling people she didn't understand when people spoke to her in Secwepemctsín. Nora was Dave Twan's niece, and she had never learned Secwepemctsín because her family was Dakelh (Carrier). And she grew up on her family ranch at Alexandria and not in the ʔEsdilagh community, so she didn't know Dakelh either.

So I guess the girl from Esk'et heard Nora telling people she didn't understand when someone spoke to her in their Indigenous dialect, so she copied her. My dad was really upset, and he bawled me out in case I done it. He said, "Don't ever be ashamed of who you are or your language. Don't you ever say you forgot!"

But I didn't think I would, I told him. It's not my character. I'm not a real good speaker of the language, but I speak it. My mom and dad spoke it, but my dad spoke English most of the time. If he had to, he'd speak Secwepemctsín.

I remember shortly after Lenny and I were married, somebody spoke to me in Secwepemctsín, and I answered them back in Secwepemctsín. Then they said, "So you didn't forget your language then!"

I said, "How could I forget it? Once you learn it, you never forget it." But it's true. Some people do forget their language when they marry white.

Ironically I never got around to teaching my own kids Secwepemctsín. I guess because Lenny spoke English all the time and I had nobody to speak Secwepemctsín with, I never thought of speaking it to the kids. Let them learn English first. I was going to teach them Secwepemctsín after, but you just never did.

🦩

I was pregnant with our fifth child that summer living above Savona, and in the fall Somavia moved us down to one of his lower-elevation ranches along the Merritt highway because he didn't want us to be stuck on the mountain over winter with a bunch of kids and me expecting a baby. The new place was a sheep farm known as the MacDonald Ranch.

Lulu was born that winter on February 6, 1962, in Kamloops, and we were the only ones in the big nine-bed maternity ward in Royal Inland Hospital. So we got lots of one-on-one attention from the nurses. Lulu had little fat cheeks so the nurses started calling her Lulu, like the comic strip character Little Lulu. So the name just stuck, and we kept calling her Lulu after that. We named her Charlene Cecilia DeRose, but she's Lulu forever.

LULU: When I was nine or ten, our teacher Mrs. Henderson at Wright Station Elementary School wrote "Charlene" on the blackboard and told me I had to use that name from now on. I said, "Why?" She said, "Because it's your name." That's the first time I knew my name was Charlene. I was in grade 4 or 5, but I never knew my name was Charlene before that. I knew my name was Cecilia, but I never knew my first name.

22

On the Move

We spent the winter at the MacDonald place along the Merritt highway just south of Kamloops. Then in the spring something didn't go Lenny's way and he had a temper tantrum and just up and quit. He'd heard about a job to run Art Lavington's old ranch in Nazko for this American couple who had bought the place. Art had told the new owners that Lenny would be a good guy to run the ranch because he knew the country. So away we went to Nazko, and Lulu was a baby.

They were building a new log house up at the old Lavington place, and when they hired Lenny they promised we could stay in the new log house once it was finished. So we went out there and were living in two little cabins. We cooked in one and slept in the other, and there was a small creek running between the two cabins.

DEDE: I remember living in the cabin at Nazko. We got some plastic fish and we had this creek, and we put the fish in the creek.

SONNY: I remember those big plastic fish. I put mine in the creek and it floated away. Those plastic fish must have been meant for a bathtub or swimming pool but we never had a swimming pool, so I turned mine loose.

CECILIA: When we got to Nazko, the new owners quit working on the new log house they were building for us to live in. In the fall I told Lenny, "It doesn't look like we're going to move into that house for the winter so we might as well move out before the winter sets in." Because it was hard living in two cabins. They were quite a ways apart.

So we moved to Quesnel. Lenny's sister Pat lived at Red Bluff and she knew of a house nearby that was up for rent, so we moved in there. Lenny went logging for the winter, setting chokers up toward Wells. He stayed in camp all week and would come home on the weekends.

Meanwhile I was pregnant with our sixth child. Rosaire Wesley DeRose was born on March 31, 1963, at G.R. Baker Memorial Hospital in Quesnel. That was the end, thank God. We had six kids in six years, and I probably would have ended up with twenty kids if not for birth control.

Wes was so sickly the doctor told us Quesnel was too damp an area for him, I guess with the Fraser River and the Quesnel River coming in. He said, "You'll have to move to a drier climate," so we went to Meldrum Creek. After that he was never sick again in his life.

DEDE: This was probably the hardest time for Mom as a mom. I was in grade 1, and we lived in a shack in Red Bluff. And Mom had to keep the house super clean because Wessey was so sickly. And she hitchhiked to the hospital every day to see Wessey because he was in the hospital all the time.

And one time he came home from the hospital and brought something back with him, and we all caught it. So we were all in the hospital. And Mom had migraine headaches and there was no medical insurance program.

Dad was working in camp, and when he'd come home he'd shoe horses all day at the racetrack and train racehorses to make extra money to pay the doctor bills for Wessey. And they were just so broke.

When Mom hitchhiked to the hospital every day to see Wessey, the neighbour lady Kay Favre would watch the rest of us while Mom was away. Kay and George Favre lived next door.

It was too much. So Mom went to the doctor, and the doctor told her she better get on birth control. But Mom said, "I can't do that, I'm a Catholic." And the doctor said, "I don't see God here helping you."

Above: Baby Wesley and me.
Below: Lulu helping Wes to walk.

CECILIA: Yeah, he said, "I don't see the priests and the nuns helping you here."

DEDE: And the doctor called Dad, and he told Dad he needed to move because it was killing Mom. Mom was eighty-three pounds. And I came

home from school one day and Mom was in bed. She had a migraine. Dad was on the phone calling from camp to our neighbours next door, so I ran down there and told him that he had to come home because Mom was crying. So he came home and we moved right away.

The doctor told Mom she should have a beer every day and take a nap every day, and Mom said, "I can't do that, I don't drink and I have six kids." And he said, "Your six kids are going to have a nap every day." So we had naps every day for years till Mom got better.

The doctor was special. He made house calls to our home to see Mom.

CECILIA: He lived at Dragon Lake and he popped into the house before he went home.

DEDE: And he told Dad, "You need to take your wife on a holiday." So Mom had to farm us all out. I had to stay home in the house because I was going to school. So this lady named Bea from Mom's church came and looked after me, and they took Sonny and the twins to Kyé7e's house, and I don't know where Lulu and Wessey went but they all got farmed out to different places, and Dad had to take Mom on a holiday. Doctor's orders.

Wesley, DeDe, Denny, Lulu, Sonny and David in Quesnel.

Then we moved to Meldrum Creek right after that. I'd finished grade 1 and Wessey was a year old.

Meldrum Creek, 1964–1966

CECILIA: Lenny's friend Eugene Johnson had a sawmill at Meldrum Creek, and Lenny went sawmilling. Gene had built four houses there, so we had a nice big house to live in, with running water and plumbing. So we stayed there for a couple of years.

Denny, David, Sonny, DeDe, Lulu and Wessie on the stairs at Meldrum Creek.

David, Wesley and Sonny amuse themselves next to their house in Meldrum Creek.

DEDE: We got to bring our two horses with us to Meldrum Creek. A pony and a buckskin. And that's where we got to meet the Turleys, the Meldrums and the Hunts. They all went to school with us, and most of us eventually got into rodeo.

When we were small, Mom made all of our clothes until we moved to Lac la Hache the second time. In all my school pictures I'm wearing the clothes Mom made. She didn't make the boys' pants, though, but she made all of our shirts and all of my dresses. And then when I was Stampede Princess she made all of my suits. All my Stampede stuff.

CECILIA: I don't know where I found the time …

DEDE: When we were living at Meldrum Creek, the Chilcotin priest Father Brown insisted that Mom send Sonny, David, Denny and me, two of the Turley kids and two of the Meldrum kids to catechism at St. Joseph's Mission. Mom didn't want us to go, and Dad didn't want us to go, but Ed Turley kind of talked Dad into it. So off we went to live in the mission just like Mom had. It was similar treatment getting separated from our family and having religion shoved down our throats. But it was better for us than it was for Mom.

CECILIA: But they had the whole school to themselves. School was out.

DEDE: There were about thirty to fifty Indigenous kids who weren't status kids who lived off-reserve. I guess Father Brown was worried we weren't going to be strong Catholics, so he opened up the school for two weeks for two summers in a row for us to take catechism. Mom didn't want us to go but Father Brown insisted. But she never sent Wessey and Lulu. She just sent us four older ones.

Mom used to have church in our house at Meldrum Creek, and Father Brown would come and Mom would rearrange our living room like a little church. And he would stand up and preach to maybe ten adults and a bunch of kids.

CECILIA: Most of the people around Meldrum Creek were Catholic.

DEDE: Then Mom would have cookies and stuff after. That's when Father Brown got this brainwave that he needed to send all of us to residential school for catechism.

It shows how much influence the Catholic Church had over people, even though Mom didn't have to—we were non-status, but the guilt and peer pressure.

We got a settlement last year for our residential school experience. But ours was called "day school" even though we were in the residential school. So we didn't get the $40,000 settlement that those in residential school got, but we got a day school settlement.

CECILIA: Taking care of Wes's health issues was expensive. There was no Medical Services Plan in those days and the doctor bills were piled sky high. Ranch wages were so low, so the only way we could pay our bills was for Lenny to go logging and sawmilling.

DAVID: I remember when we were at Meldrum Creek, we came to Williams Lake at Halloween and Dad took us out trick-or-treating. It was a day early. He got us all dressed up in costumes and we went around and trick-or-treated and nobody said nothing. Then about an hour later all the kids started coming out trick-or-treating. Maybe they were worried all the treats would be gone if they waited any longer.

In the spring, Sonny, Denny and I were down at the creek below the house, playing in the water, and Dad told us not to go down there. When Dad come home and seen us down playing at the creek again, he comes storming down there and gives me and Sonny a whooping. And Denny ran off into the trees. We were only four or five years old. And Dad took off after him. About five minutes later you hear "Waaaa!" Dad caught up to him.

And that stupid little pony we had, Blondie.

CECILIA: Everybody came and rode Blondie.

DAVID: And she had a little colt and we cornered her in the barn and she kicked Denny right in the head and he had a big black eye.

We started school at Meldrum Creek, and they failed us. We had a hootenanny teacher. And all we did all day was sing and play and draw pictures.

The DeRose kids made lifelong friendships at Meldrum Creek, where eighty per cent of the kids rodeoed. Back row, left to right: Clark Turley, Willie Meldrum, Annie Turley, Jack Meldrum and Mickey Turley; middle row: Jesse Hunt, Ivan Meldrum, Sonny DeRose, David DeRose, Denny DeRose, Ray Woods, Gary Hunt and Kenny Wilson; front row: DeDe DeRose and Bev Meldrum.

We didn't do any English. In that photograph of us kids at Meldrum Creek, 80 per cent of us rodeoed.

CECILIA: We were two years at Meldrum Creek with Lenny working in the sawmill so we could pay off our medical bills for Wes. Then once we got our bills all paid, Lenny went back ranching. In 1966 we moved to the 130 Mile on Highway 97 north of Lac la Hache, where the Dingwall and the Wright families put their two ranches together and called it the Wright Cattle Company. We were there for a year, then we went to Big Creek for two years.

DEDE: That was probably the best thing we ever did was go to Big Creek, because Dick Church treated Dad like his son. And he got Dad to start his own herd. And when Dad would have his little temper tantrums, Dick could talk him out of it because Dad had so much respect for him. Dick was also a really good horseman, and Dad had lots of respect for men who were good with horses. Dick was calm and quiet. He never got rattled. So Dad respected him and we stayed there for two years.

DeDe is in the centre of the school photo. David, Sonny and Denny are in the front row at Wright Station Elementary School where they attended for one year before the family moved to Big Creek for two years.

LULU: Mom and Dad got less careful with their children later on. By the time we got to Big Creek, Wes and I fished all day long at the creek. I said to Mom, "We were gone all day fishing, and when I went to school Wes was down there by himself fishing, and you never once came and checked on us." And she said, "Yeah, I knew you wouldn't fall."

SONNY: Yeah, because Wes came back with that big trout he caught.

LULU: And Wes talked for a long time about this big, big fish he'd seen. And we all thought it was a fish story. He'd go fishing every day and finally he caught that great big fish.

CECILIA: When DeDe was ready for high school in 1969, we went back to the 130 Mile because we didn't want to put her in the dormitory. DeDe had just finished grade 6, and that's as high as the Big Creek school went. Martin Hamm, the school superintendent, came out and told us if we stayed at Big Creek, DeDe would have to board in Williams Lake or take correspondence.

DEDE: When it was time for me to go to high school, they didn't want to put me in the dorm because of Mom's residential school experience, and because Dad didn't have a mom. They were both adamant. They didn't want to hand me over to someone else to look after me while I was going to school, and they didn't want me to take correspondence either because I wasn't very diligent. Mom and Dad really valued education, even though neither of them had a very high education.

23
Back to the '30

When we were in the Chilcotin working for Dick Church at Big Creek, we were trying to figure out how to get DeDe boarded out so she could go to high school. Either she could have stayed with Nene Twan or we could put her in the Columneetza high school dorm in Williams Lake. But once we got her boarded out, then Sonny would be next, and we'd have to board him out too. And then the twins. They're all a year apart.

When we finally got the job in Lac la Hache, we didn't have to board any of the kids out. So moving to Lac la Hache was the best thing we ever done, because we were there until Wessey graduated. Until the last one graduated. And then the ranch sold and we left.

DeDe was twelve years old when we moved back to the '30 and we put her in Lac La Hache Elementary for grade 7. The elementary school at Wright Station only went up to grade 6, so the rest of the kids went there. Sonny was in grade 6, the twins were in grade 4, Lulu was in grade 2, and Wessey was starting grade 1. The next year DeDe took the school bus to 100 Mile House for secondary school, and the rest of the kids eventually followed.

There was no school bus running as far as our place when we first got there. So we had to drive all the kids to Wright Station, and DeDe caught the bus from there to Lac la Hache. Then they extended the bus run to the 132 Mile, and our kids could catch the bus in front of our home.

DEDE: Dad had a pattern. He'd get something in his head about an employer and he'd quit. He'd come home and tell Mom, "I quit." And Mom would have to start packing.

When we moved to the '30 for the second time in 1969, it didn't take long for Dad to get mad about something. He came in the house and told Mom, "I've just about had enough around here."

And Mom said, "You can quit, but I'm not going anywhere." She said the kids needed to be in one place long enough to finish school. So he didn't quit and we stayed and we all graduated from there.

LULU: Mom got so used to moving, she'd leave half her things in boxes. I don't think she unpacked some of the boxes until they got to the River Place in 1983. Stuff like her good china and little figurines people gave her when us kids were born. Stuff she didn't need every day.

SONNY: The River Place was a big house so there was lots of room for Mom to unpack her stuff she kept in boxes.

CECILIA: The house at the '30 we had lived in three years earlier was a wreck when we got there again in 1969. So we had to clean it up before we could move in. The previous people had used the downstairs of the house as a barn.

DAVID: There was like a foot of shit on the basement floor. It took a couple of weeks to clean it up. The previous tenants lived upstairs in the house and kept the steer calves in the basement, and milked their cow down there right next to the big stove.

Our ranch at the '30 (130 Mile on the Cariboo Highway 97) was exactly halfway between Williams Lake and 100 Mile House. We lived there for fourteen years, the longest we ever lived in any one place.

CECILIA: We liked it at the '30 because we were kind of alone there with our family. The Wright Cattle Company ranch ran from the 127 Mile to the 130 Mile, and the boss would just come up once in a while from Vancouver and stay in the big ranch house at the '27.

The Wright Cattle Company owner was Bill Downie, a fancy bookkeeper down in Vancouver. But he didn't know nothing about ranching. His wife was a Wright, a sister of Gertrude Wright, who ran the ranch for many years with her husband Bill Dingwall. They were the ones who knew ranching. Then they had to retire.

Bill Downie had three kids, an older son and daughter, who were serious people who done what they were supposed to, and John, the baby of the family, who was in charge of the ranch. He'd come up to the '27 and stay in the big house there for a few days or a week, then he'd go back to Vancouver. Most of the time he was in Vancouver.

And John was a playboy down there. They wanted to get him out of town, so they'd send him up to check on the ranch. But he didn't know nothing about ranching either. And he'd try and think he did once in a while.

DENNY: But John did good too. I liked him. He's a good guy. He just phoned me the other day. We got along with him. We still get along with him.

DAVID: John was always really good to us.

Working at the Mission Again

CECILIA: With all my kids in school, I started working at the mission again. Martha worked there too, and she and I worked together again in the kitchen until it finally closed for good in 1980. By the 1970s they had a chef doing the cooking and the union was in. So they had real food and the kids could wear their own clothes.

Mostly orphans were there, or kids whose families spent their winters in the bush or meadows. Whatever excuse.

Then, once they closed the school at the mission, kids from the reserves kept staying there in the dormitory and they started busing them to public schools in Williams Lake. So we'd pack their lunches for them with a drink and fruit. Lunches were made every morning before the buses left for town.

DEDE: When I was in high school I remember coming home from school to an empty house and feeling sad when Mom worked at the mission because she'd always been home when we got home from school. My favourite days were her days off when she was at home because we'd come into our house to the smell of homemade bread and baking. I also remember dreading weekends because our house wasn't the same when she was at work and we were at home.

Mom was well liked by the staff at the mission. She worked hard and never complained. Mom worked there with Auntie Martha, Auntie Irene (who was a junior boys' supervisor) and Auntie Spic (who was in the laundry room).

LULU: Mom would sometimes bring leftover school lunches home. Every one of the lunches had a sandwich and a package of Dad's Cookies. I'd never seen Dad's Cookies before. We always made our own cookies at home.

Don't Mess with My Kids

CECILIA: One time John Downie and his wife Patti came up for branding and brought their wealthy friends from Vancouver with them for a holiday.

DAVID: They often brought along their rich and famous friends from Vancouver.

CECILIA: So at branding time John and Patti and a whole bunch of their Vancouver friends rode horses from the '27 up to our place at the '30 because that's where we done all the branding. That was a wild thing in itself. Anyway they unsaddled their horses and put the saddles all along the fence. Lulu and Wessey were just starting school.

The next day they drove up because it was raining, and all the saddles were still on the fence where they had left them the day before. I was away working at the mission when Patti came to our house and bawled out Lulu and Wessey for not getting the saddles in out of the rain.

So when I got home, they were sitting in the house and looked so sad. I couldn't figure out what was the matter. "What's going on?" I asked. "What's the problem?" They said Patti was just there and bawled them out for not bringing the saddles in out of the rain, and she called them "pea heads." Patti didn't come up with John to the ranch very often, but she was there that one time and she thought she should act like the boss's wife.

So I loaded the saddles into my car, drove down the road to the '27, took the saddles out of my car and dumped them on her porch. Then I swung the door open, knocked on the door, and Patti came to answer. I told her, "Here are your saddles. You can bring them in and take them wherever you want, but don't you ever call my kids pea heads again." I said, "You guys rode down there and unsaddled your horses and put the saddles on the fence. It was up to you to look after them. My kids aren't the hired man here," I said. "My husband's the hired man. You speak to him."

So I said it to her straight. "Who the hell's your hired hand? It's not my kids. And don't you ever call my kids pea brains again."

Patti was standing there. "John, come and get this crazy lady out of here!"

But John wouldn't even move. He stayed in his front room. "You got that Indian lady mad, you deal with it."

No, my kids always came first. If anybody had anything to say about my kids, they had to come to me. Even the teachers.

DENNY: We did a lot for that ranch for nothing, eh. We were all hired hands, but unpaid.

I Finally Get My Driver's Licence

CECILIA: I was pretty old when I got my driver's licence. I got it shortly after we moved back to the '30 in 1969. I was thirty-five or something when I finally got brave enough to go for my driver's test.

Marlene Trim was our neighbour, and Lulu and her daughter Anmarie chummed together. That's how we met. One day Marlene told me, "Cecilia, you've gotta get your driver's licence!"

I had no licence and was driving my kids to 105 Mile House for swimming lessons, and into 100 Mile for groceries. So Marlene and I met there and she said I should get my driver's licence. So we worked on it until I got it.

DEDE: Marlene taught Mom how to drive. Marlene was the head nurse in the 100 Mile hospital. There's a funny story about her and Dad going riding— she got her bra hung up on the saddle horn and couldn't get off her horse. Marlene challenged my dad on a lot of his sexist opinions, and she's the reason Mom started to become more independent.

DENNY: I never got my driver's licence until I was eighteen. I drove all the way down to Montana and back for the high school rodeo finals without a driver's licence. We had some other friends with us. Back in them days you didn't need it. We drove all over the ranch all the time. And it was right on the highway. Our ranch was right in the middle between Williams Lake and 100 Mile. Thirty miles either way.

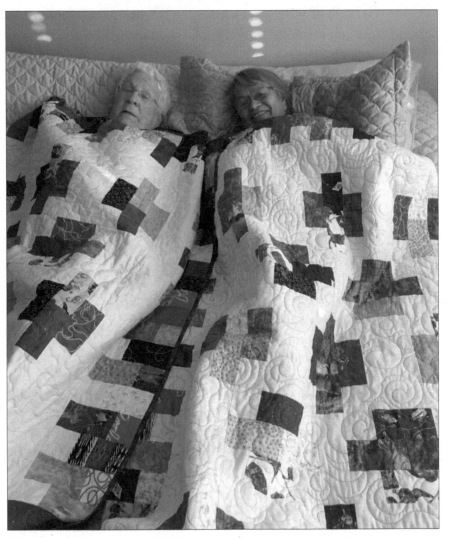

Marlene Trim and I get comfortable under our brand new quilts.

Lenny's Mom

CECILIA: Lenny's mom, Millie DeRose, was a high-toned English lady. She wasn't real English but she tried to act English. She left Wells for Vancouver before Lenny was in school, then she married a German guy and moved back to the Cariboo.

I think we were still at Alkali when she came back to work for the school board in Williams Lake as a janitor for School District No. 27. It must have been after Lenny and I got married. Then we moved to Circle S shortly after.

She came back with her German husband. They had a house in Williams Lake across from Marie Sharpe Elementary School. Her husband was a builder, so he built a house and they moved in and lived there.

DAVID: None of us kids liked her. I remember before she died she'd come around us lots. I remember her coming to visit us once at Big Creek. Then she kept coming to visit us at Lac la Hache.

CECILIA: She wanted to move in with us at the '30. Her builder husband had died by then, so she was alone. Her daughter Pat had a house in Quesnel, and Millie moved in with them for a while. But she didn't get along with Clarence,

Millie holdng Wesley when he was a toddler in Quesnel. She abandoned Lenny and his family when he was five years old living in Wells. Then she moved back to the Cariboo after Lenny and Cecilia got married. But Millie didn't approve of Lenny marrying an Indigenous woman.

Pat's husband. So she moved out and wanted to move in with us. But there were eight of us in that little house down there at the '30 and there was no room. So Lenny told her she'd have to pull up her trailer or something. Because she wouldn't be able to hang with us in that little house. Eight people. And she was such a clean fanatic.

DEDE: My grandmother was racist and was against my dad marrying my mom because she was Indigenous. She was also racist toward us and we were not allowed to go into her house. My mom's simple answer to the way we were treated by her was: "If she knew us, she'd like us." Mom never let it get to her.

My grandmother came to visit us at Lac la Hache shortly before she died. She apologized to Mom for mistreating her and us. She brought us chocolates—probably the only gifts we ever received from her.

I remember my dad crying at her funeral when he and I went up to view her body. I also remember not understanding why he was crying, because we never saw her and I never felt she liked us. Of course, now I understand that Dad never recovered from being abandoned by her as a little boy, and he held hope until she died that she would come back and be his mom one day. I didn't dislike her, though.

(Mildred Maude Dixon DeRose Elderkin died in Quesnel on April 6, 1972, at age sixty-eight.)

We Lose Felix

CECILIA: Martha and I were working at the mission when our youngest brother Felix got killed in a tractor accident at Alkali Lake. It must have been in June 1971.

Felix was working at Gang Ranch, and when he came home for the weekend to my mom and dad's place at Esk'et, they hardly had any wood left. So he got a couple of Wycotte kids to go with him. They borrowed the brand new tractor the reserve had just bought with power steering and went up the road to our family meadow to make wood in there.

They were coming down the steep hill before you get to the reserve, and Felix looked back when he got to the bottom to see if the guys were okay riding on top of the load. He was going pretty slow, and when he looked back to check, all of a sudden over he went. He got pinned under the tractor and died practically instantly. With the power steering he had oversteered it and it tipped.

Felix was just twenty-four years old when he died. The first of our brothers to go.

24
Leasing the '30

After working for the Wright Cattle Company for a few years, we had the opportunity to lease the '30 off the Downie family and run our own cattle there. We had already started our own herd at Big Creek with Dick Church before we moved back to the '30.

DENNY: We brought our own cows to the '30 when we went to work for them, and we already had our own horses. We had everything. Then we got more cows when we took it over because they got rid of their cattle so we had to get more animals to bring the numbers up to what it should be.

We were still in high school when we took over the ranch. We must have leased it for the last five or six years we were there. We worked for John for five years, but he was never around so we basically run it ourselves during that time. Once we leased it, he'd still show up once in a while.

CECILIA: Once we leased the '30, we were on our own. I mean, John would come up and visit. He still had the big house at the '27. The '27 and the '30 were all one ranch. So they'd come up to the big house and just be up there. The Downie family would still send John away from the city once in a while.

DAVID: The first year when Dad went down and paid the lease on the place, me and Sonny and Denny went down with him. Old Bill Downie said, "This is the first time I've seen this ranch make money." John Downie would be helping himself to whatever.

CECILIA: Yeah, John was always good with us and he'd invite us down to Vancouver and he'd take us all over the city. Take us to the fanciest hotel for supper. He'd take us out on his boat, over to the island and all over. He'd just entertain us the whole time we were down there.

DENNY: He had a big fancy yacht. He was a good guy. His wife Patti was okay. We never had much to do with her.

CECILIA: Patti was okay until she called my kids pea brains. She called them chicken brains at first, but when I got up there she changed it to pea brains. When I went over to beat her up for calling my kids pea brains, she was hollering to John, "Get this crazy lady out of my kitchen!" And John wouldn't even move.

I Loved the Ranching Lifestyle

Everything changes. Growing up as a kid, we only had horses. No tractors. Then at the '30 we had tractors. We started out with loose hay, then square bales, then round bales. I think on the big ranches they made silage. At Big Creek, Dick Church was right up with the modern times. I think in the end he had round bales.

But I wouldn't do anything else but ranching if I had to do it over again. I really liked that life. Those cows can't answer you back, or those horses. So you work with them. Sometimes they get ornery and sometimes they won't drive where they're supposed to go. But they end up going.

I'd help Lenny calve heifers and cows and stuff if they were having problems. You know, chasing cows, moving them from pasture to pasture and then up on the range. Once in a while we'd go up on the range, once or twice a month, just to move cows around.

Sometimes the bulls all gather together and get lazy and just stay together. So you go up there and stir them around and stuff. Bring salt, drop it here and there. Move the cows and bulls around. Stir them around so they're not lying under the trees all the time. The bulls can get lazy and want the cows to come to them.

Yes, we done all the work with the kids. Lenny was the only one getting paid when we worked for John Downie and Wright Cattle Company, but the rest of us all done ranch work. But when we took the lease on the '30, we ran the ranch as a family.

LULU: When Wes started school, Mom went back to work in the kitchen at the mission. And the boys would do the outside chores. They'd always feed the big herd of cows before we got on the school bus. And then we'd come home at night and do chores again. We all had chores. Mom would make our breakfast, put it in the oven and leave at five in the morning to go to the mission, and Dad would be working at the sawmill already.

SONNY: Dad worked at Starline Cedar Mills at Lac la Hache. He worked at cleanup and was the night watchman. I don't know why he wanted to be night watchman. Because then he made Mom go down there and feed him supper at nine o'clock.

CECILIA: Yeah, I'd go down and take supper to him every night.

SONNY: Before we went to school we'd milk the cows. We had four or five milk cows. And the boys each had their own cow to milk.

LULU: We always had pigs and chickens, and one time we had geese and sold the eggs, and sold the milk. The boys milked the cows and DeDe and I would strain the milk and make the butter.

SONNY: You know how we made butter the first time? We put all the cream in a gallon jar and we'd sit and watch TV and shake it, and pass it to the next guy. And we'd be shaking it away. Shook it and shook it and shook it. Then we looked at it and I remember it just surprised the heck out of me the first time it started to turn into butter. Then we finally got an electric butter churn.

CECILIA: That was a treat. Those gallon jars with the motor on top.

LULU: We had a hand-cranked butter churn at first because Brad Perry boarded with us. That's how his mom paid our mom for him to board with us. She loaned us her hand-cranked butter churn.

CECILIA: One of those square gallon jars. That's what she gave us. Then we had to turn it on top.

LULU: Then we got an electric butter churn. We'd wait until we got two gallons of cream, then make the butter and wash it out. Mom sold the milk, but we never sold the cream. But we sold butter.

CECILIA: I don't remember selling butter but we must have.

DEDE: As the oldest child and with Mom working, it was my job to get everybody up and out the door with their lunches. I often had to cook dinner when I got home, so I was super busy. Lucky for us, the bus would honk when it went by heading north, where it turned around at the '32, and we knew we had about five to ten minutes to get up the hill. Sometimes I had to carry Wes and someone else would carry his boots. It was crazy because we were Dad's crew and I was Mom's cook when she was at work.

LULU: I'd get up and go to the barn and do the saddle horse chores, then head back to the house to clean up after breakfast. If we were late we'd have to quickly run from the barn to the house and up the hill to the school bus, and we didn't have time to change our shoes. We tried to but often didn't have time. We did our chores every day. Mom and Dad would be gone to work, and we never missed the bus.

CECILIA: They didn't like missing school. A lot of kids would miss the bus just to miss the bus, but my kids had chores to do and then catch the bus. They didn't like missing school because they'd miss their friends.

DAVID: The bus driver, Dick Munro, had to go down past the '32 and turn around, so he'd honk the horn when he went by. So we knew it was time to get in the house. Denny and I would come out of the house wearing the same clothes, so one of us had to change. Because Mom used to buy us the same colour shirts and clothes. We'd come out of the bedroom and go up the hill to go to school and we'd be wearing the same shirt. Piss us off and we'd have to go back and change. I didn't mind being a twin but I didn't want to look like that husband-and-wife team that dress the same and walk down the street.

Sonny always got one colour and me and Denny got the other colour. Same style, just different colours.

DEDE: When I graduated from high school in 1975, I worked at the mission along with my mom and three of my aunts for a short time. Mom and Auntie Martha were in the kitchen, Auntie Spic was a janitor, and Auntie Irene was the junior boys' supervisor. That was before I went to work at the Cariboo Friendship Centre. I worked there a couple of months, but I couldn't handle the boss.

CECILIA: He was a former army guy.

DEDE: Mom could work for him, but I was scared of him. I worked at the mission with Bev Sellars. That's how come we're friends. Cecilia Michel was the head cook, so when the mean guy wasn't there we had so much fun.

When Mom was little and was home for the summer from the mission, a horse ran away and she fell and knocked all her top teeth loose. So after that she didn't ride very much.

When we were kids at Meldrum Creek, our pony Blondie took to bucking. So Mom got on that horse and gave it such a licking. Then when we got back on, she was good.

Then when we moved to the '30 the first time in 1966, Mom's sisters talked her into going to an all-girl rodeo in Quesnel. So they entered her in the cow riding. And she broke her tailbone. She came home and the bathroom in our house at the '30 was in the basement, so she had to go outside and walk all the way around. And Dad said, "You want to rodeo, you pay the price!" So she had to cook and she had to clean, and Dad said, "If that's what you want to do, then you pay the price." So there she was doing laundry and everything with a broken tailbone.

CECILIA: Yeah, I didn't get no sympathy. Yet when he broke his arm or leg, it was different. He was helpless and couldn't move or do anything.

DEDE: At the '30 we had loose hay and fed with teams for a while. We would feed, then load up the sleigh with hay for the next day, then go home. So we loaded up our hay and were going home. It was winter and it was cold. About thirty below Celsius. We were all on the sleigh and Dad decided to stop and check a beaver house, so he jumped off the sleigh. He was walking out on ice and stepped on the thin ice covering the beaver run, and the ice broke and he fell in up to his waist.

Mom was sitting on the sleigh holding the reins to control the team, and we were all on the sleigh. And we were all watching and we were laughing because it was so funny. When you're kids you don't know about hypothermia. Mom said, "You kids quit laughing!"

He crawled out of the creek and he got in the sleigh, and Mom made a pile of hay around him so he wouldn't freeze. She was so mad at us because we couldn't quit laughing. We were laughing at him because he fell in the creek.

CECILIA: It was so funny. Lenny just went to check the beaver lodge and hit a beaver run and broke through the ice. The ranch had a trapline that an old guy used to trap.

DAVID: The old trapper guy would take turns taking each of us boys us out, teaching us how to trap.

DEDE: One time Dad was riding and he got bucked off and landed on his head. He had a severe concussion and ended up getting shipped to Kamloops. That time we didn't laugh. He had surgery and the doctor told us he will either be happier or less happy when he recovers. And he was less happy.

And he was already hard to get along with. It really shifted his personality, because he used to be happy-go-lucky before he hit his head. I was in grade 8 or 9, and he was in the hospital for a while.

After that he didn't ride much. He would tell us, mostly the boys, where to move the cattle. He was the paid work hand, but if he didn't have to, he didn't ride. We were his crew.

Feeding a Ragged Stranger

LULU: When I was around ten years old living at the '30, a guy knocked on the door. He was quite grubby and wanted to talk to Mom. She was working in the kitchen and she came to the door. "Can I split some wood for food?" he asked. "I see you've got a big pile of wood there and I haven't eaten for days."

Mom said she didn't need any wood split because she had six kids to chop wood for her, but she went back to the kitchen and made a big batch of sandwiches for the guy to take with him.

When someone asked Mom if she wasn't worried this person might just keep coming back for more, she just shrugged. "You never know. He might have been Jesus."

That's the kind of person Mom is.

Lac la Hache Is Still Like Home

CECILIA: Lac la Hache was our home when I was a kid. Moose Meadow was up in there above Wright Station. That's where our family mostly grew up.

DAVID: Moose Meadow wasn't far from the '30. All of our experiences growing up as teenagers and young adults were all right there at the '30. You know, our hard work ethic. We lived right on the highway, so when we first started rodeoing, all the cowboys and cowgirls spent the night and stayed there. Even when we pro rodeoed, a lot of the guys would camp there.

CECILIA: Yeah, they'd stop in and stay overnight. Our floor would overflow with sleeping bags. And it wasn't a very big house.

DENNY: I still see Lac la Hache as home too. I drive up here to the Cariboo from Kamloops and hit the end of the lake and it feels like home. My wife Cam and I built our first place at Lac la Hache. We must have been there five years. Our sons Kyle and Denver were born in Williams Lake and the other two, Ryland and Gavin, were born while we lived at Lac la Hache.

LULU: We weren't rich growing up but we had everything we needed. Our family travelled together and we were a very close family. Our parents provided for us.

More kids than I can count came and lived with us. Ricky Nelson and Tom Alphonse stayed with us for years. Mom and Dad always had an open door where people were welcome as long as they pitched in.

25

Working for School District No. 27

When they shut down the mission for good in 1981, I went to work for School District No. 27 in Williams Lake. We were still living at the '30 and Wessey graduated from high school that year. Alan Haig-Brown hired me as a language and culture teacher for the three high schools in Williams Lake.

Alan started out as a schoolteacher in Esk'et and eventually became the head of Indigenous education for School District No. 27, covering Williams Lake, 100 Mile House and the Chilcotin. He hired Slug to teach Secwepemctsín at Crescent Heights Elementary School in Williams Lake. That's where all the Sugarcanes went to elementary school.

Then Alan wanted someone to work in the high schools in Williams Lake, so he hired me. I was based in Columneetza Senior Secondary and also worked at Williams Lake Junior Secondary and Anne Stevenson Junior Secondary. They wanted someone to teach Secwepemctsín language and culture. So I taught in the three high schools, with a class in each school. Of course, one of my first jobs was to learn how to read and write Secwepemctsín. That's one thing they never taught us in the mission. They didn't even have a Secwepemctsín alphabet at that time.

So, besides being a language teacher, I was a counsellor to make sure the Secwépemc kids knew what they were supposed to be doing. To encourage them to be something or become something. To help them get into the right programs or find the programs they wanted. I didn't know anything about high school, so I had to learn in a hurry. It was different from the schooling I'd experienced at the mission. There we did everything as a group. But the kids at the public school had many more choices than we had.

I liked Alan. He was good. He was living with Maria Myers then, a Tŝilhqot'in woman from Yunesit'in, and they had two daughters, Helen and Linda. When he'd taught out at Esk'et, he was living with a Secwépemc woman there. He had two boys, William and James, from a Kwagiulth mother. Then he moved into town and got with Maria.

A Language Teacher with a Greater Presence

—Alan Haig-Brown

Cecilia's mother and father were special. I think her mom, Amelia Dick, was born at the old village near the mouth of the Tŝilhqot'in (Chilcotin) River.

Cecilia and Lenny raised a remarkable bunch of kids. DeDe raised good questions as an educator and did good work when she came to work in the school district after NITEP (the Indigenous Teacher Education Program at the University of British Columbia). She then went on to more remarkable success in Kamloops.

In my mind, Cecilia was the pivot generation as the person between Amelia and Matthew Dick and DeDe and her siblings. When Cecilia worked as the Shuswap (Secwepemctsín) language teacher, she also served as a safe go-to for many kids. She had a room that she shared with a Tŝilhqot'in worker just off the main hallway in Columneetza Secondary School.

She was often working on a craft project in there, and kids could drop in and chat or just hang, like a little bit of home in the craziness that we call high school. Cecilia was a gentle presence with a warm laugh that lifted all who were in touch with her. The language teaching was important, but it was that greater presence of a woman who had survived and rode all adversity as effectively as any of her sons rode a bronc, or her daughters competed in their rodeo events. And always, that laughter!

Back at Esk'et, Cecilia's mother Amelia was a force to be reckoned with from that log house in the middle of the reserve. I didn't know that Matthew was on that legendary Alkali Braves hockey team. He was always very kind and direct with me. I enjoyed talking with him. He had the kind of gentle that comes from a deep sense of self.

There were a number of people who held those positions as language teachers and counsellors, and Cecilia was among the first that I hired after my position was developed by school trustees Phyllis Chelsea and Diana French in 1975. Together with the elementary Indigenous support workers and language teachers, there were about eighteen staff when I left in 1986.

Dora Grinder was my first partner working in the high schools. When she left, Patsy Grinder came as a Tŝilhqot'in language teacher and we worked together. Like if my Secwépemc kids came in for counselling and I wasn't there, Patsy would take over. We shared each other's students. We worked with all the students, Tŝilhqot'in, Secwépemc and Dakelh. Yes, we shared our students, so they could go to any one of us.

When I started working in the school, Boitanio Mall had just come in. So it didn't take too long for the kids to start hanging around the mall. Every day I had to go down there and gather them up and bring them back to school.

I worked for a number of different principals in the three high schools in Williams Lake. I got along with all of them. Three bosses. I liked John Dressler very much. He was my favourite.

I enjoyed working with the kids. When they got smart I'd say, "I've got six kids at home. I know exactly what your mind is thinking."

LULU: When Mom taught school as a Native counsellor, a lot of the white kids went to her for counselling too. They could tell her anything. Kids always knew they could trust her.

Basket Making with the School Kids

CECILIA: Besides teaching Secwepemctsín to the kids in the school, we taught them stuff about Secwépemc culture. Like how to make qwllin (birchbark) baskets.

When I was growing up we never made qwllin baskets at home. We just watched our mom do it. She showed us how to take the qwllin off the trees, cut out the patterns for the baskets, staple them all together, then sew them with t'séllpep (spruce roots).

There was an old lady in the village who was disabled. She always stayed on the reserve and could never go out. So my parents took the qwllin off the trees and gave it to her, and she'd make the baskets they needed. And my parents would trade cloth or material she couldn't make herself for the baskets she made. She was Isabel Johnson's mom. Though she was disabled, she was a perfect basket maker. And they'd give her t'séllpep and qwllin and she'd sew the baskets with the roots. Like the baskets in my collection, t'séllpep around the sides and along the top.

Some birch grows in the high country above Alkali, but mostly we collected qwllin out at Horsefly. We'd just go out there and camp, because Horsefly was one of our main places for berries and qwllin and stuff like that. I don't know if they fished salmon at Horsefly, because the salmon would come up there too.

Long ago they had big underground houses up at Quesnel Lake. At one of our culture camps there's a deep depression that looks like it was a big meeting place. There's a tree growing in the middle of it now. It was an extra-large underground house and looks like a meeting area. They must have camped up there all winter by the look of it.

We'd start the kids out in the classroom using paper to practise making the qwllin baskets. Then we'd take them out to Horsefly in the bus, and I'd show them where to find the right kind of birch trees and how to take the qwllin off the trees. We'd go in May or June when the sap was running. Then, back in the classroom, they'd use the qwllin they harvested to make their own baskets.

I'd show them where to find the right kind of birch trees and how to take the qwllin off the trees.

Once you take the qwllin off the tree, it automatically wants to roll. So you have to keep it flat by putting something heavy on top of it to weigh it down. Once it curls and dries it's hard to uncurl, so you want to keep the qwllin flat from the start. When it's flat you can cut out the patterns you need for the baskets. Then you staple it and sew it together.

We also showed the kids how to collect the t̓séllpep by digging around the spruce trees and pulling the roots up. And we showed them other stuff out there. Like where to find the berries, and how birch wood is good for firewood and qwllin is good for kindling. We always kept the white bark we took off just for fire starter.

26

Our Rodeo Family

Most of the time we tried to go to rodeos just for the kids' sake. For their entertainment. Because they worked on the ranch and never got paid nothing. So we'd go to the Little Britches Rodeos when they were young, then high school rodeos when they were older, and then the Indigenous rodeos. Alkali had one, Sugarcane had one and I think Soda Creek had one.

DEDE: We always went to rodeos if Dad wasn't haying or doing something on the ranch.

DENNY: We started Little Britches Rodeo in Williams Lake when we were six or seven. We were steer riding. Then we started going to regular rodeos when I was twelve or thirteen.

All eight DeRoses at the Alkali Rodeo. Left to right: Cecilia, Lulu, Russell Arnouse, Denny, Wes, Lenny, DeDe, Sonny and David. Photo by Don Wise.

In high school rodeo I did all the events. Bull riding, bucking horses, roping. After high school I picked bareback as my specialty. That meant I didn't have to pack a horse with me. I roped in high school and stuff.

LULU: We all started in Little Britches Rodeo before high school. Just the ones that were close. 100 Mile and Barriere were both big ones. Then we started high school rodeo, and that was a big enough thing for the family. The older kids all started at the same time. You have to be in grade 9 for high school rodeo. Then Wes and I just waited until we were high school rodeo age. I just did barrels and goat tying in high school.

DEDE: When we were in Peter Skene Ogden Secondary in 100 Mile House, we went into high school rodeo. And Mom and Dad were both really involved with the rodeo club. We didn't have a lot of money so we just used our ranch horses. But we had good ranch horses, so we started entering. Dad coached my brothers in bronc riding and bareback. So Sonny and David were bronc riders. And Wessey and Denny were bareback riders. And Dad coached them.

Dad knew some ladies who barrel raced, so he put Lulu and me in barrel-racing clinics, or he'd drive us to their houses and we would practise in their rodeo arenas. So I went and learned from Iris Wright and Dee Watt.

DAVID: In the evenings after we had done our chores at the '30, we were feeding yearlings in a pen right in front of the house. Then me, Denny, Sonny and Tom Alphonse would jump on the steers' backs and ride them. We were fourteen or fifteen years old, and they'd be nice while they were in the herd, but once they got away from the bunch they'd buck our asses off. And we'd just do that for two or three hours every night. That's how we practised steer riding. We'd do that in early fall when they came in. In the winter the frozen cow turds were hard to land on, but the spring was the worst. The cattle pen was pure mud, and when we'd land in there we'd be covered in shit. We'd have to come in the basement door and change before we went to school.

Rodeo Mom

DEDE: Mom packed our wooden camping box full of food for the rodeos. Cooked chicken, potato salad, buns, cereal, etc. She also made sure we had our big tent and our bedding. Mom was a master packer, and we had all the comforts of home when we camped.

CECILIA: One year we had the one-ton pickup. So we just put a tarp over the top of the stock racks and put our beds in there. So instead of camping out, we stayed in the back of the truck with our cookstove at one end. We really had it good that year.

DEDE: When we started competing in rodeos, all of our rodeo friends knew they would find a hot cup of coffee and a sandwich or meal at Mom's camp. Our camp was always buzzing with company with people laughing and talking around Mom's campfire. She loved it, and everyone loved her. In fact, she still hears from her rodeo kids who refer to her as their rodeo mom.

Mom would sit in the stands and cheer for everyone. She said everyone was her favourite. When we loaded up to go to a rodeo, we'd pick up kids who needed a ride along the way. And if we had a spot in our trailer, we'd haul their horses for them too. Mom and Dad did a lot for our rodeo friends who became our rodeo family.

We were competing in rodeo and we also had 4-H projects one year. Dad told us we needed to choose what we wanted to do, one or the other, because we didn't have time to do both. We all chose rodeo even though we did well in 4-H. That's when our lives got super busy, because we had to practise at home, do all the chores and help with the ranch.

The Italian Stallion

DEDE: There were many times when all six of us entered in the same rodeo. Dad got the nickname the Italian Stallion from the rodeo announcer as he ran from end to end at the rodeo arena, helping each of us as much as he could.

CECILIA: The announcer used to call him that, the Italian Stallion. I can't remember the announcer's name. He announced for all the high school rodeos.

DEDE: Mom sat in the stands and cheered. She left the coaching to Dad. However, she also told him when she thought he needed to let up. Dad wanted us to do well but sometimes was too intense.

Our Long Rodeo History

DEDE: Our family has a long history in rodeo. Our xpé7e (grandfather) Matthew Dick used to have racehorses and mountain racehorses that he entered at the Williams Lake Stampede. Dave Twan, who adopted Dad as a •

young teen, rode the mountain race and other daredevil rodeo events. Dad was also a rodeo champ.

CECILIA: Lenny rode broncs for a short while after we were married but then he quit because he had a family. There was no insurance in case he broke a leg.

DAVID: Dad won the saddle bronc at Williams Lake Stampede in 1955, then exactly thirty years later Sonny won it 1985.

Lenny DeRose Takes the Ribbon

—Sage Birchwater

The July 9, 1949, *Quesnel Cariboo Observer* reported that twenty-year-old Lenny DeRose of Narcosli took first place in steer riding at the Quesnel Rodeo. His 276 points topped second-place winner Louis Bates of Williams Lake, who had 268 points, and Bob Williams of Hope, who came third with 267 points.

Lenny placed second in the prestigious Best All-Around Cowboy competition in that rodeo, with 1,261 points, behind Maxine Mack of Alkali (2,370 points). Louis Bates was third with 1,054 points.

The Williams Lake Stampede

DEDE: Dad worked at the Williams Lake Stampede every year so he didn't have to pay. He liked to work on the racetrack, and one year he supplied the calves for the calf-roping event.

In preparation for our annual trip to the Williams Lake Stampede, Mom made all of us homemade western shirts. Sonny and Wes had the same colour, Denny and David matched, and Lulu and I were matching. And if Mom had some lace, she'd put it on our shirts. Then when we got to town we'd go to Tony's Leather Goods and they bought all of us new cowboy boots and sometimes new hats too.

CECILIA: Tony Borkowski, the owner of Tony's Leather Goods, was a shrewd businessman, but he was very generous with us. He'd give us a good discount. Maybe because we had to buy so many.

DEDE: We never missed a Williams Lake Stampede, no matter where we lived. Mom and Dad put up our big old white canvas tents at the Stampede and set up our kitchen. Dad worked at the stampede, so that got him in for free. Admission for Indigenous people was free in those days, so Mom would walk in with Sonny and me, Lulu and Wessey, and Dad would have to pay for David and Denny because they didn't look First Nations.

Lenny with his grandson Tyrell Bates at the Williams Lake Stampede.

CECILIA: They were fair. They were blond.

DEDE: They'd walk in the white gate, and Mom would walk us four in through the Indigenous gate. We got through the gate, but we weren't allowed to camp up the sidehill with Kyé7e and Xpé7e because that was the First Nations campground, so we parked down below. And then we would spend all day collecting beer bottles from around the Squaw Hall, and we'd sell them and go for carnival rides all night. This is when we lived at Meldrum Creek and Big Creek.

Squaw Hall was built in the early 1950s to keep the Indigenous and the white people separate. First Nations people weren't allowed in the white dances at the Elks Hall in town, so Squaw Hall gave them someplace to have their own dances. It was there until 1975. That's where we had our high school rodeo dance. And there were beer bottles flying. But that was probably the last year it was up. I was Stampede Princess in 1976 and I talked about Squaw Hall in my speech.

The Irish Sweepstakes

CECILIA: I had a horse in the Irish Sweepstakes. I never did win it, but I got close. Mr. O'Donovan used to sell tickets. He was from Ireland and was working at the mission as the steam engineer with Willie Alphonse. And then he married the Indian agent's daughter. They lived at the mission when I worked there.

DEDE: One night Mom got a telephone call, and she started yelling, "DeDe! DeDe! Come talk to this guy for me!" I thought something was wrong, somebody was hurt or something, so I hesitantly took the phone and Mom ran and got a piece of paper and pencil. When Mom got rattled she couldn't speak English, and she knew the guy didn't speak Secwepemctsín.

The guy was phoning to tell Mom she had drawn a racehorse in the Irish Sweepstakes. Mom always bought tickets for the Irish Sweepstakes but she never thought she'd ever win.

Holy! Our lives were upside down for a while until the race finally ran. Sadly, Mom's horse scratched. However, she still got a big cheque.

CECILIA: It wasn't very much but it was a lot to us. Maybe $1,400.

DEDE: She spent it on much-needed dining room chairs for the family. Eight of them. And she put a down payment on a motorhome so we could use it to travel to rodeos. I think it's important because it shows that she spent all of her money on us and didn't spend a dime on herself. That's how she rolled. If we were happy, she was happy.

CECILIA: It was good to win something, but if I won the big pot, it would have been better. Joe Bob at Sugarcane won the big one when we were living at the '30 the first time. That would have been 1966. He lived high on the hog for a few years, but then it caught up to him. He didn't last long after that.

The High School Rodeo National Finals

DEDE: Denny, David and I were the first to qualify for the National High School Rodeo Finals in Gallup, New Mexico, in 1975. The following year David went to Sulphur, Louisiana. Then Denny and David qualified the next year in Montana. Wes went to the nationals all four years he entered. He was an amazing rodeo athlete. We have a great picture of Dad hauling his all-around saddle from the BC high school finals over his shoulder. Dad and Mom were super proud of all of us and our rodeo accomplishments. Most of all we had fun and made lifelong friends thanks to the sacrifices Mom and Dad made so we could compete.

After learning the ropes in high school rodeo, we all continued to compete and stayed involved with the sport one way or another. There was the Interior Rodeo Association that later became the BC Rodeo Association, the Vancouver Island Rodeo Association, the Indian Rodeo Association, local jackpot rodeos and eventually, for my brothers, the Professional Rodeo Association. It was our family's happy place.

When my sons were old enough, we were back at it. First with steer riding, then in high school rodeo. Matt was BC's student president for the rodeo club, and he won the bareback riding in his last year of high school rodeo. Tyrell competed in the bull riding. All of their friends called Mom and Dad Kyé7e and Xpé7e.

Like they did with us, Mom and Dad travelled near and far to cheer their grandkids on. If they couldn't watch, they expected a telephone call updating them on how the boys did. If it was late and anybody needed a place to sleep, everyone knew they were welcome at Mom and Dad's house. They also knew they'd be fed a hot breakfast in the morning before they headed out.

Once Mom started working in the school system as a language and culture teacher, she also became the high school rodeo club sponsor. So whatever school she was in, she'd drive the students to meetings and attend the meetings herself.

When Wessey died in 1984, we had a rodeo scholarship put up in his name. All six of us had been really involved in high school rodeo. Denny was the student president for the rodeo club, then Wessey was the student president, and Lulu was the student secretary for the whole province. So Mom and Dad knew a lot about high school rodeo.

The high schools in Williams Lake relied on Mom to be involved as a sponsor teacher for the kids in Williams Lake. And Mom would even drive up to Quesnel with some of the kids for high school rodeo meetings.

Cutting Horse Champ

LULU: One of my claims to fame was winning the BC Cutting Horse Association's first youth cutting competition they ever had in 1977.

Len Monical from 100 Mile was a big cutter. Then they started up a youth association in 1977 and Len was our instructor. He had a couple of Wendell Monical's boys, me and maybe one other girl. So we all took cutting, and he had a youth cutting program and he trained us all.

I won the first cutting championship there. That year I was in the top five ladies and top five youth.

Skill and Artistry

—Sage Birchwater

The cutting horse competition is a specific category of ranching and cowboying artistry, designed to show the skill of a horse and rider to separate a single cow from a group of forty to fifty animals, and keep it from returning to the herd.

Competitors are given a choice of up to three animals they can pick from, and they score the most points by the degree of difficulty they demonstrate. For instance, they get a higher score by choosing an animal deeper in the herd over choosing one on the outer edge of the group.

Four other riders are in the arena to help with the process. Two hold the herd back and two will keep the selected cow from running away and turn it back into the herd.

The Boys Go Pro

SONNY: I started my pro career in 1981 after being runner-up the year before in saddle bronc as an amateur. I went pro from 1981 to 1984.

I took a year off from pro rodeo in 1985 after Wessey died and went back to amateur again. That's the year I won the saddle bronc at the Williams Lake Stampede, thirty years after Dad won it there in 1955.

I actually had a pretty good rodeo season in 1985. I entered the Williams Lake Stampede as an amateur and won the saddle bronc, and won saddle bronc for the Interior Rodeo Association and went to the North American rodeo finals in El Paso, Texas, and came third in saddle bronc.

I went pro again in 1986 and was in eighth place in Canada when I got hurt pretty badly in Brandon, Manitoba. Broke my arm and landed on my head and got a serious concussion.

When my rodeo career was over, my wife Tracy and I raised bucking horses out by Springhouse. Horses we raised made it to the world finals for twenty years straight. One or two of our horses bucked in the national finals. One horse was voted second best in the world a couple of times.

DAVID: I went pro in '82 and was pro for two years. I don't know how long Denny and Sonny went. Longer than me because I ended up disabled. And I got married too. My wife Deb didn't care if I rodeoed. She let me go where I wanted to go. She was a barrel racer. And we started going out when we were in grade 10. She lived in Merritt and we met in high school rodeo.

But I made my goal. My goal was to be a professional bronc rider. We still have lots of really good friends we rodeoed with.

DENNY: I did pro rodeo for three or four years in bareback. Then I went back to amateur. Then I retired. It's a pretty rough sport, but it's fun.

LULU: I competed in the BC Rodeo Association for a couple of years, then I moved to Alberta with my husband Rudy in 1985. He was a stock contractor there and ran Trails End Stock Contracting Company for many years. So as stock contractors, instead of paying entry fees at the rodeo every week, we got paid to be there. My career changed. From a shot in the dark at possibly winning, to being paid. So we rodeo stock contracted for quite a few years.

Celebrating Twenty-Five Years of Marriage

DEDE: In 1981, after Wes graduated from high school and I graduated from university, we kids decided to host a surprise twenty-fifth wedding anniversary celebration for our parents.

Sonny and I were living in an apartment in Williams Lake, and the other four were still living at home. Because there were only land lines, I would telephone down to the '30 to make plans over the phone. Even though Mom was "supposedly" deaf, she knew something was going on, so the surprise wasn't such a surprise after all. She got super excited and did what she always did when she got excited: she sewed. She made beautiful western shirts for all four of the boys and dresses with jackets for us girls.

LuLu and I took Mom and Dad to town and bought her a beautiful dark pink dress and a suit for Dad. They looked dapper. We even had corsages and boutonnieres for our family. We went the whole distance to show our appreciation and adoration for the hard work and sacrifices they had made to raise us.

We all contributed to the party, booked the Longhouse, got a band and caterers and contacted their wedding party and long-time friends. We tried to keep the guest list to three hundred people, the Longhouse's capacity, but far more than three hundred people came from across BC. In attendance was our extended family, our rodeo family, and Mom and Dad's long-time ranching friends.

Everybody had a blast. Mom and Dad's wedding party sat at the head table. All six of us gave a speech about what it was like being Mom and Dad's kids. Wes gave the final speech. He said, "Mom and Dad kept trying until they got the perfect kid. When I was born, they knew I was perfect and they didn't need to try anymore!" Everyone howled with laughter. It was so funny.

We danced until the wee hours of the night, and Mom and Dad had a blast. I don't think I've ever seen Dad happier or prouder.

PART 5

Empty Nesters and Later Years

27

The River Place

We lived at the '30 for fourteen years. That's the longest we ever lived in one place. Then a couple of years after the last of our kids had finished high school, the Wright Cattle Company was sold to Wendell Monical in 100 Mile House, and we moved to the River Place in Macalister.

DEDE: Wessey graduated from high school in 1981, the same year I graduated from university. Then Wessey went to college in Sheridan, Wyoming, because he had all kinds of rodeo scholarships. He was the BC High School All-Around Cowboy in 1981.

When the Wright Cattle Company sold in 1983, Mom and Dad stayed in the white house at the '27. Then they rented a house on Fircrest in Lac la Hache. Then they moved to Macalister near McLeese Lake.

CECILIA: We got our mail in McLeese Lake, but our house and property were in Macalister beside the Fraser River. We bought that little place in 1983 and moved up there from Lac la Hache. We had a few acres there and were there about seven years. Alfalfa fields, a single-storey ranch-style house, a shed, a hay barn and a big garden. Lenny was particularly proud of the big row of sunflowers he grew there at the edge of the garden.

I was working for the school district then and Lenny was working for the Starline Cedar planer mill in Williams Lake, owned by the same people who had the sawmill at Wright Station in Lac la Hache.

Wessey's Death

DEDE: The year Wessey died, in 1984, he was the bareback champion of the BC Rodeo Association. Nobody could believe it when he died. It was so sad. Friday night of Thanksgiving weekend. It was a big blow for all of us, but Dad took it the hardest. We couldn't even do family pictures after that, because he said our family wasn't our family anymore. He said that for a few years.

Then the grandkids started coming. He already had Cody and Matt when Wessey died. And Kirsty and Ty were born right after. Dad took it really hard. Sonny took it really hard too. Dad was really mad. Mom had to get somebody in to talk to him because he was so mad. Wessey had been driving without his seat belt on.

CECILIA: Lenny said he was the one who should have died.

DEDE: And Xpé7e (Grandpa) said that too. My sister and I had an apartment in a townhouse in Williams Lake, and they brought Xpé7e into our house and he just sat there and cried and cried. He was in his early eighties. He said, "It should have been me." Because he had Parkinson's.

CECILIA: But it's not your choice when to die. It's the guy upstairs that decides.

DEDE: Mom and Dad were living at the River Place at Macalister when Wessey died. Wessey had a bedroom and everything there. He had gone to college and he came home and rodeoed here, following the BC Rodeo Association circuit all that summer. And he won the bareback riding and was going to go pro in the spring. He was working at the Blockbuster Video store, and he'd gone to the show with a couple of kids from rodeo, and they went to a party at Chimney Lake and were driving back. But he had no one in there with him, thank goodness.

Wes DeRose and me. Wes was poised to go pro the following rodeo season when his life was cut short at age 21 in October 1984.

CECILIA: I think he just forgot how the Chimney Valley Road turns. I think he forgot how sharp the curve was.

DEDE: Dr. Peter Gooch lived right above there. And he heard the crash and ran down. Wessey was still alive, but he knew he was going to die, so he held him until he died. Then I saw Dr. Gooch about ten years ago at the Bridge Lake Stampede. He had a summer place at Bridge Lake, and he saw my son Tyrell, who died three years ago, and Tyrell looked exactly like Wes. So Dr. Gooch asked, "You don't happen to be related to Wes DeRose?"

"That was my uncle," Ty replied.

Then Dr. Gooch said, "I was with him when he died."

So Ty came and got me. I knew Dr. Gooch was with him when he died. Then Dr. Gooch told me, "I always felt badly about that."

I asked, "Why did you feel bad?"

He said, "Because he died."

I said, "We always felt happy knowing that you were there because if he could have lived, then he would have lived. He was with a doctor when he died. So it couldn't have been better."

Dr. Peter Gooch with Tyrell and his son Wyatt at Bridge Lake. Photo credit: DeDe DeRose

He said, "Well, that's not how I always thought you looked at it."

So I took a picture of him and Tyrell and showed it to Mom.

Then the other day my girlfriend Jo-ann Archibald, the chancellor of the University of the Fraser Valley, said she wanted me to come as chancellor of Thompson Rivers University to witness for her. So I did. And this lady came up to me and said, "What's your name again?" So I told her. Then she said, "You don't happen to be related to Wes DeRose?"

And I said yes, that was my little brother.

So she said, "I went to high school with him. He was the nicest kid."

She said her family moved around a lot, which is what we did before we moved to Lac la Hache. She said when she started school at Peter Skene Ogden, Wessey came up to her and asked, "Are you Indigenous?" She told him yeah. And Wessey told her, "So am I."

She said after that, whenever there was a problem or any issues, he always checked and made sure she was doing good.

She said she was sitting in the car holding her baby when she heard he died, but she didn't know any of us because Wessey was the baby of the family, so she couldn't reach out to us.

So I took her picture and showed it to Mom. It was forty years in October 2024 since Wessey died. We're still hearing stories about how many people he knew.

Johnny and Gladys Blatchford

CECILIA: Johnny and Gladys Blatchford lived just down the road from our Fraser River place on some acreage above the highway in Macalister. They used to come and visit nearly every night. Johnny liked to come and chat with Lenny about the old times. He and Lenny had known each other for years, and they talked for hours and hours. Just about every night they'd come.

Gladys and I knew each other too. We worked together at Williams Lake Junior Secondary. I was teaching language and culture, and Gladys was the school secretary. So we knew each other from there, and she'd come with Johnny and visit just about every night, and we'd chat about everything.

Johnny was a provincial policeman in Williams Lake in the 1930s, and he liked to rodeo. That gave him and Lenny lots to talk about. Johnny was a cop at Alexis Creek in the early 1940s. Cops weren't supposed to drink and enter the rodeo. But Johnny had a snort and jumped on a bronc at the Anahim Lake Stampede. He got in trouble for it and quit the police force shortly afterwards and started ranching and raising horses at Tsuniah Lake in the Chilcotin. He was good friends with Eagle Lake Henry, a Tŝilhqot'in man who gave up his Indigenous status so he could own land. I knew his granddaughter June Baptiste Draney at St. Joseph's Mission when she went to school there for a year.

When Johnny died, Gladys went north to live with her daughter.

Getting My Status Back

I lost my status under the Indian Act when I married Lenny in 1956. Then nearly thirty years later, in 1985, I got it back again. My status is important to me because I want my kids and grandkids to know where they come from.

In our time a lot of our people didn't want to admit they were Indigenous. A lot of people who married off-reserve didn't want to claim their status. But you still look Indigenous no matter what.

They looked First Nations, but lots of them didn't want to admit they were Indigenous once they married white. They got stuck-up and looked down on their own people. But I wanted my kids to know where they were from and always acknowledge my mom and dad as their grandmother and grandfather, and my brothers and sisters as their uncles and aunts.

I don't know how come it happened, but all of a sudden in 1985 they said I could have my status back. I could never figure why they took our status away in the first place. It didn't change the colour of our skin.

It didn't make me feel different to get my status back, because I knew where I came from to start with. But it felt good to get it back.

My mom and dad felt good about me getting my status back, but my dad always asked that question: "Why did they take it away in the first place?"

Bill C-31

—Sage Birchwater

In 1985, Bill C-31 allowed women who "married out" and those who lost their status under the Indian Act by other means to apply for the restoration of their status and rights. More than 117,000 people gained or regained their status as a result of Bill C-31.

Our House Fire

Lulu and Rudy were down from the north. They had delivered a bunch of horses to the States, and they were on their way back and stopped in to visit overnight. It was November 1985.

I got up that morning and went to work at the school in Williams Lake, and Lenny got up and left for the sawmill. Lulu said she thought she could hear footsteps upstairs. But there was no upstairs in our single-storey rancher-style house. And here it was the sound of burning in the attic. We had a wood furnace, and that's where it started. There was a leak in the stovepipes.

When Lulu got up to check on the footsteps, she discovered the fire burning upstairs.

LULU: We drove down and got in there at night. Visited and went to bed. We got up when Mom and Dad went to work, then went back to bed. It was November, close to Dad's birthday (the 20th), and the breaker box was making all these weird noises. So I got dressed and went outside, and there was no snow on the roof and smoke was billowing out. I ran back in and told Rudy the whole attic was on fire.

Rudy and I started hauling things outside. We grabbed the buffet and hutch full of glasses. Got Wes's saddles out, then moved down to where the bedrooms are. Mom had been sorting out pictures so we took it all outside. In all we saved two horse-trailer loads' worth of trunks and keepsakes, and Wessey's two trophy saddles.

CECILIA: Thank God Lulu and Rudy were there. They saved a few things. She saved photographs, a few pictures off the wall and my treadle sewing machine. I told her saving the pictures was all right, but rushing around and saving the sewing machine was heavy work. You couldn't go too far taking stuff out because the riverbank was right there. The house was between the river and the road coming down from the highway. So you had to go toward the garden with the junk. After the fire we set up a mobile home single-wide trailer on the property to live in.

Lenny and I Go to Italy

In 1989, shortly before we left the River Place, Lenny and I went to Italy with his brother Roy and Roy's wife Pat. Lenny wanted to meet his relatives over there. Oh, the Italians are so friendly. You should go to Italy. They just fall all over you. They get their music out while you're eating.

We went to England first where Pat's family was from. She was Roy's war bride and he brought her back home after World War II. We were there two weeks, visiting friends who had come to the ranch while Pat was seeing her family. Then we went down to Italy through France on the train. Then by boat, then back on the train again to Rome. The pope came out and done a blessing on everyone. I finally got my sins all forgiven. It was really cool. Otherwise I'd have never got to see the pope. Because I don't think he comes out just for anything. But he came out and gave us this big blessing.

Lenny and I and Roy and Pat were with a bunch of other people on some kind of tour of Italy. Then we separated from the tour and went south to where Lenny's dad grew up at the arch of the "boot." That's where his dad's parents were from. And we met all the DeRoses down there. We didn't understand a word they said. They knew some English, but Lenny knew very little Italian. His dad never spoke it once he married Lenny's mom because she spoke only English.

We had a good time. The Italians are the most friendly, top hosts. Make you feel at home. And then they sing while you're eating. They play the violin or whatever. They know how to entertain. They're happy.

I really liked my tour around Italy. It was really good. We were gone all of August just touring. We weren't in a hurry, so that was good. I was ready to come home after a week or two, but I just hung in there. I had to do what I had to do—what Lenny had to do. To meet his relatives. Because he was never going to see them again. So I had to have my patience. But that was a trip I never thought I would go on.

It came about because Lenny's brother decided we should all go together. Their sister Pat didn't go, though. She had a bunch of kids and decided she couldn't make it.

Whispering Willows Campsite

One day we were speaking to Xatśūll Kúkpi7 (Chief) Bev Sellars and she asked if we'd be interested in running the Whispering Willows Campsite owned by the Xatśūll First Nation in Deep Creek, about twelve miles north of Williams Lake on Highway 97. She said they had a hard time getting people to stay and look after it, and she told us we could move our single-wide mobile home from our River Place property and set it up right there. This was the best thing for managing the campground because when people arrived we could see them coming in. So we sold our Fraser River property and spent ten years managing the Whispering Willows Campsite in Deep Creek for the Xatśūll First Nation.

During our time there Bev used to come and get me to teach language in the evenings to people in her community. And they kind of adopted me. They adopted Lenny and me. I was still working for the school system then, too, teaching the Secwepemctsín language and culture to Secwépemc kids.

Bev Sellars sure was good to work for when she was Chief. Lenny ran the campsite mostly, and I kept busy working here and there. Lenny loved it there. He loved BS'ing those guests. That was right up his alley.

It was really handy living right in the middle of the campgrounds because we were there all the time. Of course, some of the campers loved their fires and the campsites were along the trees. So Lenny would have to stay up and make sure they put their fires out before he went to bed.

We ran a little cigarette store there, and we had to register the guests in the little book as they camped. Lenny just loved BS'ing with those American tourists. He could BS all day and get nothing done. It didn't bother him. With me, I have to get things done first and then I can relax later. He was just the opposite. He could sit all day and BS. Me, I'd be itching to get around and get going. I was doing all my stuff. I had things to do. Tanning hides and scraping hides. Sewing buckskin, moccasins and gloves, making baskets, picking berries. I mean I had to get things done.

We did hide tanning from the beginning to the end out there. And got it soft like my mother done, so you could sew it with an ordinary needle. So I showed people how to do all that.

Bev Sellars' mom, Evelyn Sellers, and me, on the Secwépemc cultural retreat.

While we were running the campsite, I went on a Secwépemc cultural retreat for the first time. I spent a week at Canim Lake with Bev Sellars's mom, Evelyn Sellars. We done things out in the bush and had meetings and decided on different things. They gave us meals. Yeah, Bev Sellars came and got me and we had our meeting. She sure had a nice mom.

28
Moving into Town

While we were working at the Whispering Willows Campsite, this piece of property came up for sale along the Old Soda Creek Road. The property was above the Rudy Johnson Bridge and went straight down from the road above the river. It didn't have a house on it, so Lenny and I talked about it and decided to buy it and set up a double-wide mobile home there to live in. So that's what we done. We left the campsite, but oh, how Lenny missed the campsite and BS'ing with the people.

When we moved to Rudy's Bridge, he was alone there because I was still working at the school and coming into town every day. So he'd come in and BS around town. He didn't like being alone. Sometimes he got home behind me.

In 2005 we moved into town because Lenny was starting to get dementia. His doctor advised us to move in closer so he could see Lenny more often, and he was concerned Lenny might wander into the river there, or get lost in the woods.

When we moved into our house on Western Avenue, that was our sixteenth move. My husband liked moving. But his dementia kept getting worse and worse, and he'd start wandering off on me. Even after we moved to town, he'd say, "Let's go into town." And I'd say, "Give me a few minutes to finish up and we'll drive down." Well, his patience was so short he'd start walking. When he decided he was going to town, he was going to town. Now, not later. So I more or less had to drop everything when he wanted to go somewhere. For what, I don't know. Sometimes just for nothing. But that's what he wanted to do.

And then sometimes in the middle of the night I'd wake up and he'd be closing the door behind him and going somewhere. I'd have to talk him into coming back in again. And sometimes it was hard, because once he had his mind made up, it was hard to talk him out of it. Sometimes I'd catch up to him way down the road and I'd tell him to get in the car.

"No, I'm walking."

"It's a long ways into town, you can't walk all the way. Where do you want to go?"

Half the time he didn't know where he was going. Finally, we put him in a home.

You couldn't have a good sleep at night because you had to be half awake, listening to what he'd be up to. A lot of times he was good and he'd sleep through the night. I don't know if it was certain times of the month that he got restless.

He was mad about getting put into care, but there was no way I could look after him. Sometimes he'd get mad, and he was strong. When he made up his mind, there was no changing it. You'd try and go along with whatever he'd decide, but sometimes it didn't make sense. Because he'd go back into his childhood. His dad raised him and his mom left when he was five. There must have been anger at being abandoned.

Lenny died on September 14, 2010. He would have turned eighty-two that November.

He loved his sunflowers. At the bottom of his garden at the River Place he had a big row of tall sunflowers. And he always grew sunflowers at our place in Williams Lake on Western Avenue. They still grow here but not as tall as they did in Macalister.

Lenny and I had a good life. I didn't know I was going to marry him, but we did. We had six kids. And Lenny more or less raised himself. So he done his own things with his friends. But he had a lot of friends.

And he'd bring me wildflowers when he came home from riding the range. And our son Sonny used to follow suit sometimes when he was little. The first dandelion would come into the house. The first little dandelion would be sitting on our kitchen table. He took after his dad. Bringing flowers. Wildflowers.

29

Special Honours and Accolades

The Chancellor and the Honorary Doctor

by Sage Birchwater

In the spring of 2024, Thompson Rivers University (TRU) announced two significant commendations for DeDe and Cecilia. In April, DeDe was proclaimed the university's new chancellor for a three-year term, succeeding retiring chancellor Nathan Matthew, who had held the university's highest figurehead position for two three-year terms.

Then, on June 4, 2024, at TRU's convocation ceremonies, DeDe's first official act as chancellor was to bestow an honorary doctor of letters on her mother.

Immaculately attired in a green and purple gown and hat, Cecilia looked regal escorted into the hall by her son Denny. The procession of dignitaries

DeDe and Cecilia at the Thompson Rivers University 2024 convocation in Kamloops where DeDe bestowed an honorary doctor of letters on her mother. Photo credit: Thompson Rivers University.

and graduates entered the room to the sound of Secwépemc drummers and singers, and Canada's national anthem was sung in Secwepemctsín.

T'exelc (Williams Lake) First Nation Kúkpi7 (Chief) Willie Sellars read the citation, and DeDe did well riding her emotions as she confided to the graduating class that Cecilia was indeed her mother.

In fact, the whole convocation ceremony demonstrated how an institution of higher learning can be a leader promoting social change. It is significant that the university located on the unceded lands of the Tḱemlúps te Secwépemc would demonstrably recognize Secwépemc culture and tradition in the institution's highest order of ceremony. A recognition long deserved.

The Citation Read by Kúkpi7 Willie Sellars

Today we are bestowing an honorary degree upon Ms. Cecilia Dick DeRose. Cecilia of the Esk'etemc First Nation is a Secwepemctsín teacher, adviser and celebrated champion of language revitalization.

Nationally recognized as an Indigenous knowledge keeper and contributor to communities at large, her deep commitment to promoting understanding, her respect for nature and her dedication to Indigenous traditions,

T'exelc cultural ambassador David Archie and Kúkpi7 Willie Sellars join Cecila, DeDe and Denny at the TRU convocation. Photo credit: Thompson Rivers University.

values and practices have deeply impacted the healing of Secwépemc communities.

Since her experience in residential school to reviving and preserving her nation's language and culture, Kyé7e (Grandmother) DeRose has been committed to teaching future generations across the Cariboo Chilcotin School District for almost twenty years.

She is highly regarded for tirelessly sharing her wisdom and knowledge with faculty and students at the University of British Columbia, Royal Roads University, Simon Fraser University and Thompson Rivers University, and with the works of Dr. Marianne Ignace.

A prominent advocate for Indigenous voices, Kyé7e DeRose co-wrote and edited a comprehensive guide to Secwépemc ethnobotany, and created programming that preserves language and tradition as a leader of the Northern Shuswap Tribal Council skills development team. She was an Elder adviser to the Culturally Safe Dementia Care research project dedicated to supporting First Nations Elders with memory loss. In the 1980s, she sat on the Katie Ross Inquiry in Williams Lake and provided cross-cultural training for the area's hospital, RCMP and courts.

Kyé7e DeRose now teaches the Secwepemctsín language at Elder College in Williams Lake, serves as an Elder adviser at TRU and is a board member of the Spi7uy Squqluts Language and Culture Society. She also contributes her expertise for First Voices Secwépemc, an online platform for Indigenous language revitalization.

In 2018, she received the Indspire Award for Culture, Heritage and Spirituality for her expertise in teaching Secwepemctsín, as well as her handiwork with beads and animal hides, and her knowledge of traditional and medicinal plants.

Kyé7e DeRose's dedication and leadership continue to inspire the next generation of Indigenous leaders, facilitating positive change for themselves and their communities going forward.

Honourable Chancellor, on behalf of the Senate and Board of Governors of Thompson Rivers University, I am pleased to present to you Dr. Cecilia DeRose for the degree Doctor of Letters, *honoris causa*.

Many family members gathered to honour my honorary doctor of letters.

Cecilia's Acceptance Speech

Weytk. Kukwstsetsemc.

My heart is glad to receive an honorary doctorate of letters from Thompson Rivers University.

Kukwstsetsemc to TRU, Kúkpi7 Sellars and Geraldine Bob for believing I am worthy of this prestigious honour.

Kukwstsetsemc to my family and friends for joining me today. To you I say: I can't believe I'm a Doctor. Even though I've always loved learning, I aged out of residential school when I was sixteen and had to go to work at minimum-paying jobs. Today I'm eighty-nine and I'm finally a Doctor! (And I'm an "Indian Doctor" at that!)

Like my dad, Matthew, told me: "Always be proud of who you are and where you come from."

He said: "Never forget our language and culture. Speak Secwepemctsín proudly whenever you can." And that is what I've always tried to do.

When teaching my six children and my students I always told them: "We only have one arrow left. It's education. You must use it wisely because we, your Elders, sacrificed a lot to ensure you have this arrow."

To the 2024 Thompson Rivers graduating class of law: I wish you every success in your futures. I look forward to hearing about all the great and wonderful things you do.

Kukwstsetsemc.

Some Irony at the Convocation

—Sage Birchwater

Cecilia was immaculately dressed in a predominantly green robe and hat for her honorary doctorate presentation at TRU, and her daughter DeDe caught the irony right away.

"Green is not Mom's colour," she said. "She never wears green. When Mom got really sick during her first year at the mission, they fed her green Jell-O. So now she can't stand Jell-O or the colour green. It has never been her colour."

"They put me in bed at Christmastime at the mission, and they fed me green Jell-O," Cecilia confirmed. "And I've never liked it since. By Easter I got over my sickness, and I never had that problem again. I don't know what caused it."

But no matter the colour of Cecilia's attire, she looked opulent. A queen in green!

Indspire Award 2018

DEDE: It was Bev Sellars's idea to nominate Mom for the 2018 Indspire Awards. She submitted the application to nominate Mom for the award as a linguist uniquely skilled in sewing buckskin and beadwork and basket making.

Mom already had a Language Champion award from the Province of BC and the First Nations language association. She and Clara Camille were Language Champion recipients at the same time in 2011.

Indspire Awards are given out annually to outstanding First Nations, Inuit and Métis individuals who have excelled in their field in a range of categories and regions across Canada.

On November 7, 2017, it was announced that Mom would be one of thirteen recipients of the 2018 Indspire Awards for her outstanding contribution to culture, heritage and spirituality. So in November we flew off to Ottawa for Mom to get introduced to the prime minister and the federal government.

Others signing on to support this nomination included Alan Haig-Brown, author, educator and former director of Indigenous education for School District No. 27; Marianne Ignace, author and Secwepemctsín language specialist from Skeetchestn; Judge Bryan Williams from Vancouver, one of the first judges to work on land claims in British Columbia; and

Family members join me for the Indspire Awards presentation in Winnipeg in the spring of 2018.

Wendy Cocksedge, plant ecologist with Royal Roads University, specializing in non-timber Indigenous forest values.

All worked with Mom in one capacity or another in her career dedicated to teaching and preserving the Secwepemctsín language and traditional cultural practices. All five of Mom's kids and some of her grandchildren and great-grandchildren joined her in this unique honouring of her life and work.

LULU: The Indspire Awards ceremony was held in Winnipeg in the spring of 2018, and the MC for the event was comedian, actor, screenwriter and radio personality Darrell Dennis. Mom taught Darrell when he was in grade 9 at Williams Lake Junior Secondary. He was an awkward little kid at that time. He told everyone how much he appreciated Mom encouraging him to believe great things were possible for him.

DEDE: Mom was the first recipient to get her award, and Darrell said how excited he was to witness Mom receiving this recognition.

Cecilia Recognized as a Language and Culture Champion

Cecilia received a Language Champion Award with the First Peoples Cultural Foundation in 2011 after DeDe applied to have her recognized for her tireless work in language revitalization. The following, written by DeDe, appeared in the February 2015 edition of *Adminfo*, the BC Principals' and Vice-Principals' Association journal:

> In spite of attending residential school as a child where speaking her language was forbidden, Cecilia maintained her language.
>
> She worked in all areas of kindergarten to grade 12 in the public school system, teaching her language and culture to children for seventeen years.
>
> After she retired from the Cariboo Chilcotin School District, she began working for universities to develop their Indigenous language programs.
>
> Cecilia has worked tirelessly in writing and developing curriculum to teach our language and culture in an effort to ensure that the language does not die.
>
> In recent years, she has devoted her energy to Head Start programs and enjoys working with young children.
>
> Also she has devoted her time to teaching our language in the Elder College in Williams Lake.
>
> Besides being a "teacher" in every sense of the word, Cecilia has also taken courses to work as a translator for the RCMP, hospital and court system, and has attained countless certificates from institutions.
>
> Besides learning, teaching and translating, Cecilia is also the Elder who is most often asked to make buckskin moccasins and gloves, birchbark and pine needle baskets, beaded necklaces, earrings and hatbands, and beaded eagle feathers—because her work is outstanding.
>
> Her crafts have been sent everywhere across Canada, Australia, England, Japan, Switzerland, Germany and the USA.
>
> It is for these reasons that Cecilia is worthy of being recognized as a Language Champion in BC.

Cecilia Gives Secwepemctsín Names to Her Family Members

Cecilia holds up Denny and Cam's hand scripted name cards.

DEDE: In 2020, during COVID, Mom got worried about how the pandemic was going to end or if it was even going to end. She was worried because she realized none of us had Secwepemctsín names, and she figured it was her responsibility to give us traditional names.

It took her months to consider each of her family members, their personalities, likes and dislikes, and assign names. Then she made each of us an Indigenous memento to give to us when she gave us our names. She invited members from Esk'et to drum and sing, and she invited her friend Orrie

Charleyboy to smudge us and hold a Sunrise Ceremony. She also assigned three of her grandsons to assist her in speaking and four of her granddaughters-in-law to assist with gift giving.

Our names were given to us on a Family Day weekend. Everybody camped and ate together on our reserve at Lac la Hache. She gave out almost sixty names that day. It was beautiful.

DEDE'S FAMILY

Allan: **Skeleqs** (Brown Bear). Guardian of the world.

DeDe: **Tse7ekw te Spi7uwi** (Sunrise Golden Eagle). Divine Spirit giving warmth, light and life.

Derek: **Estqw Skllekstem** (Cedar Rain). Generous caretaker and giver of life.

Leah: **Stput' te Kwellr7ep** (Misty Waterfall). Messenger between the spirit world and earth.

Timber: **Tyeqwten te Tseqellp** (Majestic Fir Tree). Spiritual purifier and protector.

Jhett: **Slexlex te Tsellp** (Guardian Spruce Tree). A lucky, resilient healer and protector of health.

Matt: **Skwekw7e re Sqexe** (Sun Dog). A respected, fierce guardian who gives warmth, light and life.

Acacia: **Slexlix te Spi7uwi** (Spirit Thunderbird). A supernatural protector from evil.

Arden: **Smukwe7ce** (Sunflower). She who makes beautiful surroundings.

Brilyn: **Tsitsqw te Sulensem** (Wild Rose). A pretty flower that is a spiritual protector from harm.

Emmerence: **Sqwyilcs re Stextsin** (Dancing Tiger Lily). Spicy and pretty flower that dances, is prosperous, confident and proud.

Tyrell: **Tsekulecw te Tsicwtsecw** (Sunrise Fish Hawk). A wise, courageous and strong protector.

Aliannah: **Qné7e's Tskikse7** (Great-Grandmother's Chickadee). A curious, cheerful and social dreamer.

Wyatt: **Tsicwtseew** (Red-Tailed Hawk). A visionary hunter.

LULU'S FAMILY

Rudy: **Xpé7e Megcen** (Grandfather Moon). Protector of the family.

LuLu: **Kyé7e Megcen** (Grandmother Moon). Guardian of the family.

Travis: **Skemcis** (Grizzly Bear). A courageous, strong provider and protector of great strength.

Lauren: **Clexlix te Setekwe** (Calm River). Northern giver of life.

Arabella: **Qwiqwit te Megcen** (Blue Moon). One who embraces power.

Talon: **Yelal te Megcen** (Full Buck Moon). Full of energy. After the huge full moon that is only seen in July when the bucks' antlers are at full growth.

Payton: **Tsitslem te Megcen** (New Moon). One with stunning energy.

Rose: **Liweltsen te Megcen** (Crescent Moon). A warm new beginning with serenity and poise.

DAVID'S FAMILY

David: **Nuxwsqexe7** (Running Horse). A powerful free traveller.

Debbie: **Tukwtwetkwe** (Calm Waters). The sacred quiet giver of life.

Cody: **Kenkeknem** (Bear). Thoughtful independent bear.

Kim: **Setsinem Re Iswell** (Singing Loon). Creator of hopes, dreams and wishes.

Layne: **Smuwe7** (Cougar). He who leaps at opportunities.

Eberle: **Stekteqwtut'qw** (Gentle Fawn). She who is kind, graceful and curious.

Kirsty: **Relalkwe** (Rippling Water). A splashing giver of life.

Shawn: **Swelaps** (Bighorn Ram). A curious seeker of new beginnings.

Brettly: **Tscts'7** (Spirit Dove). The meeting of the earth and spiritual worlds.

Kensly: **Tsitsqwsul'ensem** (Wild Rose). A symbol of life and vitality.

Finly: **Xwexwne** (Hummingbird). A playful warrior.

SONNY'S FAMILY

Sonny: **Qwmu7sqexe7** (Wild Horse). Free and powerful.

Tracy: **Setetkwe Kekesu** (River Salmon). Faces challenges with determination.

Dylan: **Cseliken Qwilqen** (Great-grandchild Wolverine). Extremely adventurous like great-grandfather.

Riley: **Megcen Melemsiye** (Moon Wolf). Transformational best friend to the moon.

DENNY'S FAMILY

Denny: **Xwensqexe7** (Fast Horse). He who is free and quick.

Cam: **Stektseketkwe** (Sparkling Water). The giver of life in a sparkly way.

Kyle: **Tek-tsiqw te Xgwelemc** (Fire [red] Fox). He who is cunning, agile and clever.

Jessica: **Spegmic** (Swan). She who is graceful and kind.

Noella: **TqitQe** (Wild Strawberry). She who brings spring sweetness.

Raiden: **Tqwigwit te Xgwelemc** (Grey Fox). He who is cunning, agile and invincible.

Denver: **Tyogwten Styexyeyx** (Spirit-Power Bobcat). He who has ancient soul wisdom.

Haley: **Crelrelalltse Setse7** (Strong-Hearted Raven). She who is magical and courageous.

Austin: **Tskikse7** (Chickadee). Curious, cheerful, social, a dreamer.

Tate: **Sne7em te Kenkeknem** (Spirit Bear). One who can do anything. Gentle and strong and fierce.

Ryland: **Slexlix te Semrew** (Spirit Lynx). An intuitive guardian, guide and listener.

Elysha: **Ski7ekst Tsi7** (Northern Wind Deer). Graceful, caring, compassionate, adventurous.

Deacon: **Ckenmimelt** (Little Bear). A healer and guardian of the world.

Lennie: **Butta Sulensem** (Wild Buttercups). She is the first flower of spring.

Gavin: **Tet7i7kwem Tsikette** (Spark Firefly). A creature of light.

Jesse: **Xwelxwleqe** (Dragonfly). Communicator with the spirits.

Cecilia also gifted names to:

Lenny DeRose: **Sqwuqwyem nt'se7sqexe7** (Ghost Horse).

Wes DeRose: **Slexlixtert'se7squxe7** (Spirit Horse).

Lynn Mobbs: **Skepts te Skllekstem** (Spring Rain). A spiritual fertility for the earth.

My collection of handcrafted gifts I made for each member of the family at their naming ceremony.

30
Memories of Kyé7e and Xpé7e

When the kids were young we'd take our four oldest to my parents' place at Moose Meadow, and Lenny and I would go on a holiday. Every year we'd go visit the couple who raised Lenny at Wells, the Rivieres, who had moved down to the Kootenays. So we'd go down there for a while.

Then we'd go visit my old girlfriend, Joan Beliveau, who lived in Surrey and ended up with seven kids. We'd go visit her for a while. When she came up to the Cariboo, she'd always visit me. Then when we finally got home to pick up the kids at Moose Meadow, my mom was always glad to see us. She was ready for our holiday to be over.

DEDE: Yes, we went to Moose Meadow with Kyé7e (Grandmother Amelia) and Xpé7e (Grandfather Matthew). We never stayed on the reserve because things were getting wild then. We went up to the meadow in a team and wagon and had a blast. Kyé7e gave us little lard buckets to carry water up from the creek and to pick berries with. She told us not to talk when we picked berries because it slowed us down. That was hard for me. We washed our clothes using a scrub board. Xpé7e told us ghost stories before we went to sleep. We had a blast.

One time when we stopped by to visit Kyé7e and Xpé7e at Moose Meadow, someone had just driven over Kyé7e's dog. She was so sad. Because they never drove a vehicle and only had a team, she said, "That car stepped on my dog."

DAVID: We were pretty young, I would say seven or eight, when we came back from Big Creek and spent a week or two up there at Moose Meadow with Xpé7e and Kyé7e. Basically they just turned us loose and let us run wild for two weeks. We'd take our little .22s and shoot squirrels and grouse and chipmunks. We stayed in the hunters' cabin, and Mom and the girls stayed in the main cabin, and we just run wild. They were on that side of the creek and we were on this side of the creek.

I can remember all the mattresses were hung up from one side of the room to the other, and we hung them back up when we left.

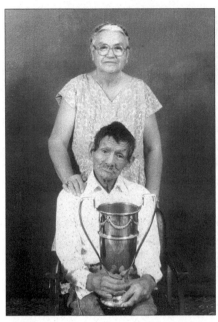

Matthew and Amelia hold the Mountain Race Trophy that Matthew's horse won many years earlier at the Williams Lake Stampede.

CECILIA: We hung up the mattresses because the rats would come in and take them over. So they had to hang the mattresses up when they left the house.

DAVID: The cabins were really clean and nice and neat and tidy. Nobody ever touched them. Nowadays it's different.

CECILIA: People would stop in and use the cabin if they needed to. Cook on the stove and stop in for lunch or whatever, because we never locked them. All the meadows up from the reserve were the same. They never locked them. They'd leave them open in case somebody needed to stay overnight. And if you burned firewood, you'd replace it.

DAVID: Another time I remember Xpé7e telling us where to go and how to read the blaze signs on the trees, because it's really tough country out there. You can get lost really easy. So they had marks on the trees, and each blaze pointed to the blaze on the next tree. You follow the blazes and it took you to different places, then you follow the blazes home again. And he'd tell us all about it and we'd just bugger off and follow those trails.

I remember him taking us out hunting. Me and Sonny and Denny. He comes back and he says, "Holy, this is the noisiest bunch of kids ever." When we headed out we tried our damnedest to be quiet, and we come back and he said, "Holy cripes, you are noisy." And we thought we were doing really good, but that's just learning how to do it.

The 18

CECILIA: The 18 is a meadow halfway between Moose Meadow and Esk'et. Sometimes when we were kids, going back and forth to Moose Meadow, we'd camp there at the 18 for a couple of days, then carry on in whichever direction we were going. The 18 is actually part of Esk'et reserve, away from the main village.

Later on, my dad built a little cabin there on the side of the meadow where the creek went through. After my parents were older and had moved away from Moose Meadow and were living in their house in the village, they'd stay at the 18 when they wanted to get away from the drinking in the village. My dad never got any sleep at Esk'et because everybody was awake at night. They'd sleep during the day and get drunk at night. At first people were just drinking on weekends, but after a while they were drinking all the time.

The 18 was just a meadow with no buildings when we were little. I think my parents used to hay it and go and get hay when they ran out down at Esk'et. Martha lives there now. The reserve built five houses there, and Martha and Bill Sure live in one of them. They built them eight or ten years ago maybe.

My dad liked getting away from the reserve. So did my mom. They enjoyed leaving the village. Then they enjoyed coming back and visiting again. But the drinking was really bad there for a while. My mom was never a drinker, but my dad would join the gang once in a while.

A lot of people at the village had nothing to do. Except my dad always liked to ride and hunt and stuff. But the people at Esk'et just quit hunting. They sold their horses and just drank and done nothing. Some of them had hayfields and put up hay. Like Jimmy Johnson and his family, they still hayed and put up hay. But the rest just let it go.

Coyote Barking

One time the kids and I went down to the 18 and stayed there for a week on our own. Just me and the kids and our dog. We went there to have a holiday. The 18 was nice and peaceful. Nobody else around.

One night we're all sitting there with no TV or power. Just a little gas lamp. All of a sudden a coyote came up to the house and started barking. Our dog just lay there on the front step and didn't lift his ear. He didn't even hear the coyote. Our ancestors always said when a dog ignores a barking coyote, that's when somebody's gonna die. And usually somebody died and you're gonna hear about a death or something.

Then we saw a light off in the distance and thought somebody was coming to give us some bad news. But it was Mike Isnardy just coming for a visit.

After he left, the kids and I were still spooked. I put the lamp down low, and we all went to bed. I can't remember who died, but somebody did.

The Last Years of Matthew and Amelia

Toward the end, my dad's Parkinson's got so bad they couldn't go to the meadow, so they stayed at the village all the time. My brother Richard was the main person looking after our dad. Richard could pack him in if they went somewhere. It was faster than having a person on each side walking with him. Richard wasn't a big man but he was strong.

Riding horses was my dad's way of having fun. He loved his racehorses when he was young, and even with his Parkinson's he'd jump on a horse and go for a ride. He'd go saddle up, and Richard would make sure his cinch was tight because he just wanted to go for a ride. I don't know where he'd go. He'd just go riding. We worried about him riding around because of his Parkinson's. But then the horse would always bring him home.

Once they moved to the village, they just sat around and didn't do nothing. My mom had a garden, but my dad wasn't a gardener. When he was still healthy, he'd plow it with a team. That's all he done. My mom done the rest.

When we were kids we had to do the weeding. She'd do most of the garden herself, because we were at the mission when she planted it. But we'd have to weed the garden when they let us out for the summer. Before we went to the meadow to hay.

Alice Belleau (Amelia's half-sister), Amelia and Matthew at their 50th wedding anniversary at St. Joseph's Mission in 1980.

DEDE: When I worked at the Friendship Centre I was asked to be the rodeo secretary for the Esk'et jackpot rodeo. So I went out early in the week to do the draw and type the program. I stayed with Kyé7e and Xpé7e in their log house in the village and put my bay mare barrel-racing quarter horse, Kay's Finale, in Xpé7e's little log barn beside the house.

I got up in the morning and went up the road to Boweville, near Springhouse, to do the draw with the judges and the rodeo stock contractor, Gus Gottfriedson.

After doing the draw I went back to Kyé7e's to get changed and exercise my horse, but my mare wasn't in the barn! A little while later Xpé7e rode up to the house window, beaming from ear to ear. He'd asked Uncle Leech (Richard) to help him saddle my mare so he could go for a ride. He told me she reminded him of his old racehorse Kitty Toy and he couldn't resist taking her out for a ride.

Kyé7e was furious. "Silly old man! You could get hurt!" But he rode away on my mare, prancing up and down the reserve, smiling and waving at everyone as he rode by. Even though he already was suffering from his Parkinson's symptoms, you couldn't tell when he was riding. He was so happy. It's a fond memory of mine.

Amelia Joe Dick

CECILIA: My mom passed away quite a ways after my dad. She ended up in Deni House (a long-term care home attached to Cariboo Memorial Hospital in Williams Lake) for about three years. I brought her some huckleberries one time when she was in there. She loved picking berries. Her mind was still good, but she died of old age. She stayed with Spic for two or three years, then Spic put her in the care home. I guess she couldn't look after her anymore. Bernard was around, in and out, but he couldn't look after her either. And Richard was always there.

31

Family Bits and Pieces

My Sister Irene

My uncle Joe used to call my sister Irene "Nurse" because she used to babysit Spic, Slug and Felix. She was the babysitter until they were all old enough. And my Uncle Joe would call her Nurse.

Then Irene actually became a nurse later on. She was the first one in our family to graduate. The first from Alkali reserve to graduate. And then she became a nurse. So maybe Uncle Joe could see something in her.

SONNY: Wasn't she one of the first Indigenous people in Canada to get a nursing degree? Before that they used to kick you out of school when you were sixteen.

I Never Liked My Name

CECILIA: Martha was the name of my mother's biological mother, and Amy was the name of my dad's aunt. So they named my older sister Martha Amy. She's just a year and two months older than me. I've only got one name, Cecilia, and I'm named after my dad's sister Cecilia.

I hate my name. I don't know why. But everybody says a lot of people don't like their own name. So I guess that's the way it is.

Uncle Richard's Last Request

DEDE: When Uncle Richard was sick and dying, he chose what he wanted said at his funeral. So he told Mom to call me. I went out there to Esk'et, and he was in his bed in Xpé7e's house. He told me to bring paper and a pencil. So I sat in there. Mom and Auntie Martha, Auntie Spic and Shirley Robbins all sat around and told stories about him. And I sat there making a list of what he wanted us to say.

And he would say, "No, you can't tell that one," and "Don't tell that story." Then he'd say, "Yeah, you can tell that story." And then he told me, "I only want you to talk at my funeral. I don't want it to go on and on. I don't want any bullshit or any cow shit. Whenever people die, they make them sound like they're so great. I wasn't that great. Just tell stories about me."

Six siblings: Spic, Willard, Slug, in the back; Martha, me and Irene in the front.

So I sat there and wrote all these stories.

At Indigenous funerals, everybody gets up and whoever wants to talk, talks.

Because he said that, Mom stood at one side and Uncle Willard stood at the other and made sure no one got the mic, and I just told his story, and that was it. And we buried him. No extra stories. No extra frills. And one of the stories he let me tell was him cutting off the heels of Martha's high-heeled shoes she got from one of Xpé7e's hunters.

Another one was how at the dances they'd paint their faces black. How they'd get all dressed up and go to dances and you'd have to guess who people were. So he said okay to that one.

It was a funny eulogy because it was only his stories.

One time he was taking hunters out, the ones Xpé7e turned over to him, and these hunters took him to Pasadena, California. They were all so amazed because he knew all the country in Dad's hunting area like the back of his hand. They never felt like they would get lost. He knew it so well.

So they took him to Pasadena, and they said, "Let's see if he's got such a great sense of direction down here." They dropped him off in the centre of the city and they drove home. And he walked home. And when he arrived back at their house, they said, "How did you know how to find your way back?"

He said, "I just watched where we were going when we came here."

So I told that story. How Uncle Richard paid close attention to stuff.

Willard, me and Richard.

Joseph DeRose

DEDE: My only memories of my grandpa Joe DeRose are that he was a wonderful, kind man. He never remarried after his wife Millie left, but he always brought us candy and loved all of us dearly. We were little when he died, but I vividly remember learning about his death because my dad was crying. It was a sad time.

SONNY: I remember Grandpa Joe DeRose. I wasn't very old. Mostly I remember that he was bald. I'd never seen a bald person before. I wasn't quite five when he died.

CECILIA: He used to come and spend time with us every summer.

Joe DeRose's Obituary
Quesnel Cariboo Observer
January 3, 1963

DeRose Funeral Held Yesterday
Funeral service for Joseph DeRose, 77, a resident of Wells for the past 29 years, was held at 2 p.m. yesterday at St. Ann's Church in Quesnel, with Father Sheffield officiating. Interment took place at Quesnel Cemetery.

Mr. DeRose had spent Christmas at the home of his daughter Patricia in Quesnel and was returning to Wells last Friday when he suffered a fatal heart attack at the bus depot.

Emergency treatment was given by members of the Quesnel Fire Brigade inhalator squad and was continued at Baker Memorial Hospital, but Mr. DeRose failed to respond.

A native of Italy, he came to Canada with his parents while still a boy. He worked on the construction of the Grand Trunk Pacific Railway and on the PGE Railway. Following completion of the PGE to Quesnel he moved to Prince George where he engaged in several business ventures before moving to Wells in 1934.

He was employed at Island Mountain Mine for 21 years, and also operated a café business in South Wells prior to his retirement about four years ago.

He is survived by his wife, residing in Vernon; two sons Roy of Fort St. John and Len of Quesnel, a daughter Patricia of Quesnel; a brother in Italy; a sister, Mrs. V. Talarico of Gilroy, California; and 17 grandchildren.

Millie DeRose Elderkin

In the Funeral announcement for Mildred "Millie" Maude Dixon DeRose Elderkin in the *Quesnel Cariboo Observer* the newspaper mistakenly identified her first name as Amelia.

Funeral Held for Pioneer
Quesnel Cariboo Observer
April 12, 1972

Funeral services were held for Cariboo pioneer Amelia Maude Elderkin on Sunday, April 9, 1972, at 2:30 p.m.

The services were held at Clayton Funeral Chapel with Rev. J. Fast officiating.

Mrs. Elderkin passed away in G.R. Baker Memorial Hospital on April 6 at the age of 68. She was born in Oxbow, Saskatchewan, and had been a resident of the Cariboo for 53 years.

Surviving Mrs. Elderkin are two sons, Roy DeRose of Fort St. John and Leonard DeRose of Lac la Hache; one daughter Mrs. C. Crocker of Red Bluff; two brothers in Ontario, T. Dixon and R. Dixon.

She is also survived by 20 grandchildren and seven great-grandchildren.

Following the services the remains were forwarded to Fraserview Crematorium in Prince George.

Nene and Dave Twan

DEDE: Nene and Dave were my godparents. I adored them, especially Nene. She taught me how to dance the Charleston. I still have the pullover sweater and travel clock she gave me. She was a kind, caring lady.

An important lesson Nene taught me: My dad always used to take a grape or two when we were shopping for groceries. I thought everyone did it, so I did it, too. When I told Nene I did that, she said, "Can you imagine if every little girl ate two grapes? There would be no grapes left for the store to sell."

I never took another grape after that, and I still think about the lessons she taught me occasionally. She was always happy.

DENNY: There's a picture of Xpé7e (Grandfather Matthew Dick) and his twin brother Uncle Joe Dick holding me and David when we were babies. Twins holding twins, and David and I got our middle names from them. The trouble is nobody knows for sure who is who, because Dave Twan was always playing practical jokes on us and switching us around.

CECILIA: He used to try and trick me. He'd switch the cradles around. But I still knew who they were. I could just tell. I could tell by their personalities.

Dave Twan, the Rodeo King

—Sage Birchwater

When Dave Twan died in 1983, the headline in his March 29 *Quesnel Cariboo Observer* obituary described him as a "Rodeo King." It said he never missed a Williams Lake Stampede and was made an honorary member of the stampede by the Stampede Association and received a complimentary free ticket to stampede events after that.

It said that in his younger days, Dave competed in the "dangerous and thrilling Mountain Race" and would do trick riding during slack times between rodeo events. The obituary concludes that Dave was the first person to do the Death Drag at the Quesnel Rodeo.

David DeRose recalls: "I remember Dave Twan telling us about riding in the Williams Lake Stampede mountain race, and when they put the new road through at the bottom of the track, he had this terrible accident. He said when he came down the steep slope, the horse went to jump the road and threw him off. And he said when he woke up in the hospital, they were picking gravel out of his chest. I guess it was just a wreck once they put the new road in. You'd come straight down and then up. So I guess the mountain race got cancelled after that."

The obituary describes Dave's mountain race recovery: "While recuperating from surgery after a mountain race one year, he cooked for a road crew ... and he was a good cook and proud of the prune pies he baked."

George and Anne Riviere

CECILIA: George and Anne Riviere were the only family Lenny knew growing up in Wells. And they weren't even related. George was kind of a half-breed. Part First Nations and part French. Métis. His wife was English but she was dark.

Lenny really enjoyed the dogsled races when he was young because George took him under his wing and taught him about the dogsledding. He also taught Lenny about horses. In winter they did dogsled racing, and in the summer they'd come to Quesnel for the horse races and Lenny would be his jockey. He was little and light then. But he got chubby after that and got too heavy.

George and Anne had a son, Rusty, who was younger than Lenny, but Rusty wasn't interested in dogsledding or horses, so Lenny became the son George could do this with.

Every summer we'd go down to the Kootenays to visit George and Anne. They moved to the Kootenays when they left Wells. Yeah, they were his real parents. And we visited them every year on our holidays. Lenny made sure to go and visit them. See how they were doing. He really appreciated them. He always said, "They raised me."

On the left, a rodeo friend of the boys, then George's son Rusty Riviere, Lenny DeRose, Sonny DeRose, David DeRose, George Riviere, Tom Alponse, Denny DeRose and Wes DeRose with his face covered.

An excerpt from the March 15, 1941, edition of the *Quesnel Cariboo Observer* tells the story of twelve-year-old Lenny DeRose competing in and winning the annual dogsled derby in Wells:

Dogsled Derby Champ

An interesting event at the Wells Ski Meet on Friday last was the boys' dog derby. The race was run over a half-mile course—from Island Mountain waste dump by way of the hospital and finished up at Johnston Bros. garage. There were six entrants and the race was keenly contested all the way. Each boy had one dog. The winner was Leonard DeRose, Eddie Snoxell was second and Eugene Johnson third. The best-equipped outfit was Eddie Snoxell's with Eugene Johnson winning second money in this class. Third best-equipped was that of Len DeRose.

This was the second year that the boys' dog derby has been run, and the event bids fair to be one of the most interesting and exciting in future ski meets.

Judges were Howard Sinclair and Tom Elliott, with George Riviere as starter.

32

Conclusion

What's Special About Each of My Kids

DEDE

DeDe is outgoing. She does her thing; she does important work. And she's always friendly. She had two sons, Matt and Tyrell, who both followed the rodeo circuit. Sadly she lost Ty in 2021.

Matt works in the mine near Kamloops. The same mine my son Denny has worked in for many years. Matt and his wife Acacia have a little ranch in Hat Creek, west of Cache Creek, and he and Acacia have three daughters, Arden, Brilyn and Emmerence, who are all barrel racers.

DeDe is married to her childhood sweetheart Allan Mobbs, and they celebrate their blended family. Allan's son Derek has two kids, Timber and Jhett. Ty's two children are Aliannah and Wyatt.

SONNY

Sonny is Sonny. He works all the time and tries to be grumpy now and then. But he does his own thing too. He and his wife Tracy have their own little place. He loves his bucking horses. He and Tracy raised some of the best bucking horses in the world on their ranch near Springhouse.

He was the first of my boys to go pro in the rodeo, and he won the saddle bronc at the 1985 Williams Lake Stampede exactly thirty years after his dad Lenny won that same event at the 1955 Williams Lake Stampede.

He and Tracy had children later in life, and they have two boys, Dylan and Riley. I don't know why he never encouraged his boys to do rodeo, because that's the only thing he ever done was rodeo. Dylan went to Saskatchewan to go to school to be a PE teacher, and Riley is working on a ranch in Kamloops somewhere. Sonny tries to be grumpy, but it doesn't suit him.

Sonny is foreman at a sawmill in Williams Lake where he's worked for forty years.

DENNY

Denny is always Denny. He's always happy. He always comes to see you. He phones once in a while to check on you. But he's always pleasant and not grumpy.

Denny married Camilla in 1985, and together they have four boys: Kyle Riviere, Denver Robb, Ryland Dennis and Gavin Lloyd. And they have six grandkids: Noella, Raiden, Austin, Tate, Deacon and Lennie.

Denny was a pro rodeo bareback rider for three years, then ended his rodeo career as an amateur. He attended Thompson Rivers University in Kamloops and got a business degree and worked at several businesses. For many years he's been a machine operator in the mine near Kamloops and he loves that work.

DAVID

David is always happy and he always has his dreams. He's always dreaming up something. Just like his dad. You know, big dreams. He's always pleasant and nice and never grumpy.

David was a professional saddle bronc rider for a couple of years but had to retire after suffering serious injuries. He drove logging trucks for a few years in Merritt, then decided to go back to school and become a schoolteacher. He got his education and master's degree from Thompson Rivers University and a master's degree from California, and taught and was principal in several schools around Kamloops, Ashcroft and the Cariboo Chilcotin.

David married Debra Ann Byer in 1982, and they have two kids, Cody Joseph and Kirsty Ann, and five grandkids, Layne, Eberle, Brettly, Kensly and Finly.

LULU

Lulu is always good. She never changes. And she never plans on ever being a big shot. She's just Lulu and will always be Lulu. She does a lot of hard work for her husband Rudy. I mean, she's right in there. Hard work doesn't mean nothing to her. What has to be done has to be done, and that's it. She's "Let's get it done and get it over with." That's the way she is.

Lulu and Rudy Ostrem moved in 1985 to Eureka River, Alberta, where Rudy was a stock contractor supplying bucking animals to various rodeos around BC and Alberta. He has three children from a previous marriage, Clint, Toni and Dawn, and in 1989 Lulu gave birth to their son Travis David. In 1991 Rudy and Lulu tied the knot and were married on May 19.

Their blended family includes Travis and his four children, Arabella, Talon, Payton and Rose; Rudy's grandchildren Darby, Dane, Dylann, Liam, Sean and Olivia; and one great-grandchild, Kohen.

WESLEY
Wessey was always so friendly. He fit in with other people like he'd been there forever. He'd talk to anybody, and everybody looked after him. And he let everybody know he was Indigenous.

DEDE: Wessey was always inviting his teachers to come out to the ranch for branding when we lived at the '30. None of us other kids did that.

What's Special About Your Mom, Cecilia Dick DeRose?

DAVID: Mom's work ethic, the same thing as my dad. Work hard, get an education. Whenever we got kicked out of school or kicked off the school bus, Dad and Mom made sure they worked the shit out of us. So none of us got kicked out very often.

Another thing both Mom and Dad told us: Don't be high-toned. In other words, don't show off; don't brag about what you are; don't put yourself above other people.

LULU: The biggest lesson Mom taught us: Nobody's better than you or anybody else. She didn't treat anybody any different, from one person to another. She treats everyone the same, whether you've got millions of dollars or not a penny. I think that's really important. She didn't treat the wealthy people from Vancouver any different than she treated members of her own family.

Mom didn't tell us about her residential school experiences when we were growing up. It was around 2013 when she first told some of the stories while speaking at the school in Eureka River. She had a really hard time telling those stories. She was obviously carrying a lot of the hurt she suffered there for a long time.

DEDE: Nobody worked harder than Mom. She set a high standard for us. If she asked us to do something, it was something she wasn't afraid to do herself. She did everything with a smile on her face and with a great sense of humour.

She also wasn't afraid to try new things. She taught herself how to play the guitar, how to oil paint. She took Italian speaking lessons, she whittled, she made wedding cakes and wedding dresses for people. She sewed our western shirts and helped the boys make their own chaps. She sat on the Katie Ross Inquiry in Williams Lake even though she did not know the justice system. She also sat on the board for the Friendship Centre. She did all of this while cooking delicious meals for our family, doing the laundry, keeping our house spotless, cleaning the chicken house, gardening and canning. I don't remember ever hearing Mom complain or say she was tired. It was a rare thing to find her sitting in the living room watching TV.

Finally, and most importantly, she encouraged us to try new things and not be afraid. She was our biggest fan. She expected perfection, modelled it and asked for it. She told us when we didn't do things up to her expected standard, but she wasn't mean about it. She'd advise us how to improve or fix things and would send us back to try again.

Mom is also the most selfless person I know. If she has five dollars and she thinks someone needs it more than she does, she will give it to them. She never expects to get it back and is always grateful if she does get it back. Money isn't important to her, nor are material possessions. Most of her house is decorated with things we or her grandkids and great-grandkids made for her. Those are her most prized possessions.

What's Special About Your Dad, Lenny DeRose?

DAVID: As a rodeo competitor, Dad told me to never quit trying. As a human being, always be honest. Hold your word. Value your word. And remember where you came from. Never walk by someone you know on the street.

DEDE: Dad's kids were always number one. He appreciated having a family so much because he essentially had to grow himself up.

Dad was a little more complex. He had a fantastic sense of humour and a wicked temper. He demanded respect for Mom at all times. Nobody was allowed to say anything disrespectfully to her or swear around her. However, he expected Mom to take care of his every need, and she did.

Dad was also respectful of everyone's situation and advised us from a young age to respect everyone. Nobody was better than anyone else. He encouraged Mom to practise our culture and speak our language. He said we should be proud of it.

Dad's greatest gift was his horsemanship. He did a great job of teaching us how to handle and read horses. If there was a place where he was patient, it was on horseback.

Dad was hard on us. There were times when Mom had to intervene because he expected too much from us. However, his friends told us that he bragged about us to them all the time. Compliments to us didn't come often, but he told everyone who would listen about how proud he was.

When he first learned he had dementia, he asked me to be sure that we took good care of Mom because he wouldn't be able to anymore. He was crying.

A Final Word from Cecilia

I'm proud of my kids. I think they done good. They've done all right. They're not bad kids. They just flow with the world. And my grandkids and great-grands are good, and they all call me Kyé7e.

My great-grandkids: Talon Ostrem, Arabella Ostrem, Emmerence Bates, Rose Ostrem, Payton Ostrem, Arden Bates and Brilyn Bates.

Afterword

—Sage Birchwater

On January 11, 2025, another great DeRose gathering was held to celebrate Cecilia's ninetieth birthday. This was organized by the twins, David and Denny, and Lulu, who travelled south from Eureka River, Alberta, with her husband Rudy to make it all happen. And they pulled out all the stops. Rented the Longhouse, gathering place of all things Indigenous in Williams Lake, hired a band, catered a meal and invited family and friends from near and far to attend.

With the manuscript close to completion, I asked David whose names we should include in an acknowledgements section of his mother's memoir. David simply swept his hand around the room, indicating everyone who had come to celebrate Cecilia's milestone birthday.

"Holy smokes, are you crazy?" I said, and David simply smiled.

People were there from across the bioregion we affectionately refer to as the Thompson Cariboo Chilcotin Central Coast. That's who we are; that's our 'hood.

So I milled about the room. The first person I spoke to was Jack Palmantier, former world champion bareback rider from Riske Creek, now in his eighties. He explained how he had recently been felled by a stroke and had to claw his way back, willing himself to get back walking again while in hospital care in Kamloops. Rodeo linked him to the DeRose family.

Next was Tom Alphonse. Tom, a member of T'exelc First Nation, was one of several kids welcomed into the DeRose household when he was a teen growing up. He recalled how he and David, Denny and Sonny honed their rodeo skills by riding yearling calves for a few hours every day. "We'd start in the lighted inside of the barn and the animal would burst out through the door into the blackness of the night. You never knew where you were gonna land."

Next was Ricky Nelson, who met the DeRose family at Big Creek when they all lived there. Then, like Tom, Ricky went to live with the DeRoses at the '30 near Lac la Hache, and was part of their rodeoing cohort. Cecilia told me later that Ricky's dad had a hunting camp at Big Creek. When the DeRose family moved to the '30, Ricky eventually showed up there too. "We always had about ten kids that would come and stay and blend in with all the rest. But they had to do chores. Milk the cows, feed the cows and horses, slop the pigs.

They didn't come there and sit around. They had to pitch in and help with the work. I think what they liked was the rodeo part. High school rodeo was a good plan because all the kids went into it."

Down the table was T'exelc councillor and former Kúkpi7 Ann Louie. The last time I saw her was on the big video screen in the Elizabeth Grouse Gymnasium at Sugarcane a few weeks before Christmas. Ann was in Ottawa with Kúkpi7 Willie Sellars to receive an official apology from Prime Minister Justin Trudeau for the illegal displacement of their community in 1860. "It's a good thing you got that done in time before Mr. Trudeau resigned," I said to her. Ann agreed. "It's all about timing," she said, smiling.

At another table I met ninety-three-year-old Dale Lefferson. Dale lived at Alexis Creek when I first knew him thirty years ago. He served on the school board during the 1980s. Before that, in his youth, he cowboyed and rodeoed with Cecilia's husband Lenny. "Dale used to chum with Lenny when they were young," Cecilia said later. "They used to travel together cowboying in the Chilcotin."

Next to us was ninety-one-year-old Shirley O'Connor. "I'm older than Cecilia too," she quipped. "They named me after Shirley Temple, who was five years old when I was born." Shirley's husband was the handyman at St. Joseph's Mission when Cecilia worked there.

There were many more people in the room. Maybe over one hundred. But you get the picture.

When we first walked into the Longhouse we were greeted by a couple of Cecilia's great-granddaughters, who instructed each guest to sign a hand drum for Cecilia with a felt-tipped marker. Close to the entranceway Cecilia's sister Spic, also known as Julia Victorine, sat with her husband Willie Alphonse. Out of the blue I asked if she also had a Secwepemctsín name. "Of course I do. It's Qe7llellken," she said. I had to prevail upon T'exelc language specialist Jeanie William to spell it for me, and she kindly obliged.

Of course, this birthday bash was to be a surprise for Cecilia. She's used to having various family members visit from out of town. So when Lulu and Rudy showed up from Eureka River and Denny and his son Gavin arrived from Kamloops, it was no big deal. Business as usual.

The guests were told to get to the Longhouse at four o'clock and the family would bring Cecilia there at five. Then they made up an elaborate scheme telling Cecilia they were taking her to dinner at the Point Restaurant. But first they wanted to stop by the Longhouse, where Cecilia's friend Butch was going to be drumming.

In this photo, I am showing Prime Minister Justin Trudeau the picture I had taken with former Prime Minister Louis St. Laurent back in 1954. "Back then I was young and the prime minister was old. Now I'm old and the prime minister is young!" Photo credit: DeDe DeRose.

"I told them I'd rather just wait in the car, but they insisted I come in with them," Cecilia told me later. "When I walked in the door there was no Butch and no drum, and all these people were there blowing noisemakers. I was surprised so many of my family and friends had made it. It was a nice crowd."

Cecilia was genuinely blown away. They had pulled it off. She walked in the door like a deer in headlights.

Kyle Larden was the master of ceremonies. He's the son of Bucky Twan Larden, whom Cecilia babysat at Alkali Lake Ranch when she worked there as a sixteen-year-old in 1951. And Bucky was also there with her two daughters.

Kúkpi7 Willie Sellars was joined by Kristy Palmantier to ceremonially drum the opening with a couple of traditional Secwépemc songs. Then he spoke about the significance of Cecilia's journey and how she has inspired him as a leader of his community and the Secwépemc people.

"I hold Cecilia close to my heart. I've been drumming all over North America in recent weeks, in Ottawa and in Washington, DC. I couldn't be happier to be home. Cecilia inspires me to be proud of who we are as Secwépemc people and proud of where we come from. Her pathway forward allows someone like me to do the work we do."

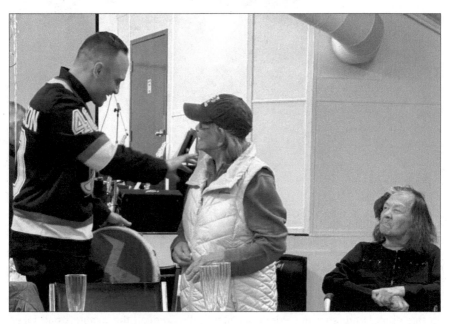

Kúkpi7 Willie Sellars greets me at my 90th birthday celebration. My sister Spic "Que7el-lellken" watches in the background. Photo credit: Kirsty Bowers.

Acknowledgements

—Sage Birchwater

The initial urging to begin this memoir of Secwépemc knowledge keeper Cecilia Dick DeRose came from her friend Barb Testawich. It was Barb who tracked me down to say Cecilia was ready to tell her story.

Quickly the posse assembled. Cecilia's five kids, DeDe, Sonny, David, Denny and Lulu, filled in the gaps of the narrative told by their mother and helped convey their family legacy. And they were joined by their spouses Cam, Deb and Tracy DeRose, Allan Mobbs and Rudy Ostrem, who all had a hand in bringing the story forward. As did friends Dawn Armes and Fay Buchanan encouraging and supporting our efforts.

Kúkpi7 Willie Sellars of T'exelc First Nation, educator and author Alan Haig-Brown and former Xatśūll Kúkpi7 Bev Sellars all added poignant parts to Cecilia's story .

Thanks to Monica Lamb-Yorski for tracking down the identity of Father Joseph Anthony Boyle, the priest who married Cecilia and Lenny at St. Theresa Church in Esk'et.

The ranching community also stepped forward to help us solve the identity of Jose Ramon Somavia, who hired Lenny in the early 1960s to manage the Whispering Pines Ranch. Cecilia recalled him as "Samlavia." But thanks to David Zirnhelt, Duncan Barnett, Mary MacGregor, Doug Haughton and Dave Haywood-Farmer, we were able to set the record straight. Kamloops archivist Mitchell Fridman and editor Meg Yamamoto also pitched in.

Thanks also to Amy Thacker of the Cariboo Chilcotin Coast Tourism Association (CCTA) for generosly providing us with a map of the region and to Sandra Hawkins for proofing and for her helpful suggestions.

Special thanks must go to Caitlin Press publisher Vici Johnstone for giving Cecilia the opportunity to tell her story, and to Sarah Corsie for her diligent work behind the scenes. And we owe much gratitude to Meg Yamamoto for her brilliant job of editing this "story by committee."

Appendix 1: Timeline

1843   Birth of Cecilia's great-grandfather Alexander Tlourtaskret Parkranaxt Johnson.

1876   Birth of Cecilia's grandfather Dick Johnson.

1885   Birth of Lenny's dad, Joseph DeRose, in Italy.

1899   Marriage of Dick Johnson and Margaret/Marguerite "Makrit" Seymour (Simo), by Father François Marie Thomas on May 12 at St. Joseph's Mission.

1902   Birth of twin brothers Matthew and Joe Dick on April 16.

1904   Birth of Lenny's mom Mildred "Millie" Maude Dixon.

1911   Birth of Cecilia's mother Amelia Joe at Esk'et on August 26.

1927   The Alkali Lake Braves hockey team starts out with Matthew Dick as goaltender.

1928   Marriage of Dave and Nene Twan in August; birth of Lenny DeRose in Prince George on November 20.

1930   Marriage of Matthew Dick and Amelia Joe on February 1 at St. Joseph's Mission, by Father V. Rohr.

1931   Birth of Victorine, first child of Matthew and Amelia Dick, in Esk'et in January.

1932   January 15–21, the Alkali Lake Braves hockey club plays the semi-professional Commercials in Vancouver; birth of Willard Dick on August 15.

1933   The Alkali Lake Braves play their final season; birth of Martha Dick (Sure), at Empire Valley on November 9.

1935   Birth of Cecilia Dick (DeRose) on January 14 at Esk'et.

1936   Birth of Richard Dick on September 30 at Esk'et.

1939   Birth of Irene Dick (Basil) at Esk'et on March 7.

1940   Willard Dick starts residential school at St. Joseph's Mission; birth of Bernard Dick at Esk'et on December 26.

1941   Death of Victorine Dick in the spring; Lenny DeRose wins dogsled race in Wells on April 15 at twelve years old; Martha starts residential school at St. Joseph's Mission.

1942 Cecilia starts residential school at St. Joseph's Mission.

1943 Birth of Danny Twan on July 25; birth of Julia Victorine "Spic" Dick at Sugarcane on September 12.

1944 Birth of Margaret Louise "Slug" Dick at Esk'et on September 4.

1946 Birth of Felix Dick at Esk'et on November 11.

1949 Dave and Nene Twan move to Alkali Lake Ranch, where Dave is ranch foreman; Lenny DeRose wins the steer riding at the Quesnel Rodeo in July.

1951 Cecilia graduates from residential school at St. Joseph's Mission in June, starts her first paid job at Alkali Lake Ranch, and meets Lenny DeRose for the first time.

1952 Cecilia quits her job at Alkali Lake Ranch in the fall and heads up to Moose Meadow with Martha, and they trap squirrels for the winter.

1953 In spring Cecilia and Martha start work as kitchen helpers at St. Joseph's Mission.

1954 Cecilia and Joan Beliveau go to Quebec on Our Lady of the Cape Shrine pilgrimage.

1955 Lenny wins the saddle bronc at the Williams Lake Stampede.

1956 Cecilia quits her job at the mission and goes to work for Hilary and Rita Place in Dog Creek; Cecilia and Lenny are married on December 1 at St. Theresa Church in Esk'et; Lenny's mom Millie moves to Williams Lake with her German house-builder husband.

1957 Thirteen-year-old Danny Twan moves in with Lenny and Cecilia for the winter; Deborah Anne "DeDe" DeRose is born on June 4 in Williams Lake; Lenny and Cecilia move to Dog Creek to work for Circle S Ranch.

1958 Birth of Leonard Richard "Sonny" DeRose on July 4 in Williams Lake.

1959 Birth of the twins David Joseph DeRose and Dennis Matthew DeRose on June 27 in Williams Lake.

1960 The DeRose family moves to Heffley Creek north of Kamloops.

1961 Lenny is hired by rancher Jose Ramon Somavia to manage a ranch above Savona for the summer; the DeRose family relocates to the MacDonald sheep ranch for the winter.

1962   Birth of Charlene Cecilia "Lulu" DeRose on February 6 in Kamloops; Lenny quits Somavia and the family moves to Nazko; the family moves to Red Bluff near Quesnel in October; Joe DeRose dies on December 28 in Quesnel.

1963   Birth of Rosaire Wesley DeRose on March 31 in Quesnel; DeDe starts grade 1 in Quesnel in September; Wesley is sickly and his medical bills pile up.

1964   In June the DeRose family moves to Meldrum Creek, and Lenny starts sawmilling.

1965   Lenny continues sawmilling at Meldrum Creek; the four older DeRose kids go to catechism at St. Joseph's Mission for two weeks in the summer.

1966   The DeRose family moves to 130 Mile to work for the Wright Cattle Company.

1967   The DeRose family moves to Big Creek to work for Dick Church.

1969   The DeRose family moves back to 130 Mile to work for the Wright Cattle Company; DeDe starts grade 7 at Lac La Hache Elementary; the rest of the kids enrol at Wright Station Elementary.

1970   Cecilia goes back to work at the mission, cooking in the dorm with her sister Martha; Lenny starts working night shifts for Starline Cedar at Wright Station; DeDe starts grade 8 at 100 Mile Junior Secondary, Sonny is in grade 7 at Lac La Hache Elementary, and the rest of the kids continue at Wright Station Elementary.

1971   Cecilia's youngest brother, Felix, is killed in a tractor accident at Esk'et in June.

1972   Death of Millie Maude (DeRose) Elderkin on April 6 in Quesnel.

1974   The DeRose family leases the '30 from the Wright Cattle Company.

1975   DeDe graduates from Peter Skene Ogden Secondary (PSO) in 100 Mile House and starts work at the Cariboo Friendship Centre.

1976   Sonny graduates from PSO; DeDe enters the NITEP (Indigenous Teacher Education Program) at the University of British Columbia in September.

1978   The twins graduate from PSO.

1980   Lulu graduates from PSO.

1981   DeDe graduates from UBC; Wes graduates from PSO; St. Joseph's Mission shuts down and Cecilia starts teaching Secwépemc language and culture in Williams Lake secondary schools; Sonny enters pro rodeo.

1982   David DeRose and Debra Ann Byer get married in Merritt on February 26; birth of Cody Joseph DeRose, son of David and Debra, on July 28 in Williams Lake.

1983   Death of Dave Twan on February 21 in Naniamo; birth of Danial Matthew Bates, son of DeDe and Danial Bates, on June 28 in Williams Lake; the '30 gets sold to Wendell Monical, and Cecilia and Lenny buy and move to the Fraser River place in Macalister.

1984   Wes is killed in a car crash on October 6, 1984, at twenty-one years of age.

1985   Birth of Kirsty Ann DeRose, daughter of David and Debra, on January 10 in Merritt; birth of Tyrell Rosaire Bates, son of DeDe and Danial Bates, on April 21 in Williams Lake; marriage of Denny and Camilla Gay Belsher on May 18 in Williams Lake; Sonny wins the saddle bronc at the Williams Lake Stampede; Cecilia regains her Indigenous status; the River Place ranch house burns to the ground in November; Lenny and Cecilia set up a mobile home to live in at the River Place.

1987   Birth of Kyle Riviere DeRose, son of Denny and Camilla, on February 2 in Williams Lake.

1988   Birth of Denver Robb DeRose, son of Denny and Camilla, on April 5 in Williams Lake.

1989   Birth of Travis David Ostrem, son of Lulu DeRose and Rudy Ostrem, on May 1 in Eureka River, Alberta; birth of Ryland Dennis DeRose, son of Denny and Camilla, on July 7 in Williams Lake; Cecilia and Lenny go to Italy to meet Lenny's family.

1990   Lenny and Cecilia start managing Whispering Willows Campsite at Deep Creek for Xatśūll First Nation; birth of Gavin Lloyd DeRose, son of Denny and Camilla, on December 18 in Williams Lake.

1991   Marriage of Lulu DeRose and Rudolf Ruben Ostrem on May 19 in Eureka River, Alberta.

1993   Marriage of Sonny DeRose and Tracy Lynn Hutchinson on May 15.

2000   Lenny and Cecilia move to the Old Soda Creek Road place above

Rudy's Bridge; birth of Dylan DeRose, first child of Sonny and Tracy, on September 4.

2002   Birth of Darby Ostrem, first grandson of Lulu and Rudy, on November 6.

2004   Birth of Riley DeRose, second child of Sonny and Tracy, on February 20.

2005   Lenny and Cecilia move to Williams Lake with Lenny suffering from dementia.

2008   Marriage of DeDe and Allan Mobbs on February 2.

2010   Marriage of Matt Bates and Acacia Margaret Hilda Oitzl on May 14; Lenny dies in Williams Lake on September 14.

2011   Cecilia wins BC Language Champion Award on July 11.

2014   Marriage of Travis Ostrem and Lauren Ritchie on August 9; the Vancouver Giants wear Alkali Braves jerseys, and DeDe buys six Giants/Braves jerseys for the family.

2017   Cecilia is nominated for an Indspire Award.

2018   Cecilia receives the Indspire Award.

2022   Birth of Kohen Basnett, son of Darby and first great-grandson of Rudy and Lulu, on September 13.

2024   DeDe is declared Thompson Rivers University chancellor in April; Cecilia receives her honorary doctorate at TRU on June 4.

Appendix 2:
Cecilia's Children and Descendants

DEDE: Deborah Anne DeRose born June 4, 1957.

Spouse: Married Allan Mobbs February 2, 2008.

> Derek Allan Mobbs born May 28, 1983, to Allan and Lynn Pozzobon Mobbs (Lynn passed away July 20, 2006).
>
> Derek married Leah Cressy Hassel August 4, 2007.
>
>> Timber Marino Mobbs born April 20, 2014.
>>
>> Jhett Franklynn Mobbs born September 9, 2019.
>
> Danial Matthew (Matt) Bates born June 28, 1983, to DeDe and Danial Glen Bates.
>
> Matt married Acacia Margaret Hilda Oitzl May 14, 2010.
>
>> Arden Margaret Cecilia born November 12, 2010.
>>
>> Brilyn Catalina Ann born October 31, 2013.
>>
>> Emmerence Mattie Mikhail born September 1, 2016.
>
> Tyrell Rosaire Bates born April 21, 1985, to DeDe and Danial Glen Bates.
>
> Two children with Ariel Tanner:
>
>> Aliannah Jocelyn Tanner born November 20, 2012.
>>
>> Wyatt Wesley Tanner born November 27, 2019.
>
> Tyrell died January 8, 2021.

SONNY: Leonard Richard DeRose born July 4, 1958.

Spouse: Married Tracy Lynn Hutchinson May 15, 1993.

> Dylan DeRose born September 4, 2000.
>
> Riley DeRose born February 20, 2004.

DAVID: David Joseph DeRose born June 27, 1959.

Spouse: Married Debra Ann Byer February 26, 1982.

> Cody Joseph DeRose born July 28, 1982.
>
> Cody married Kimberly Ann Presley June 28, 2008.
>> Layne DeRose born March 19, 2010.
>> Eberle DeRose born August 25, 2013.
>
> Kirsty Ann DeRose born January 10, 1985.
>
> Kirsty married Shawn Dale Bowers June 25, 2011.
>> Brettly Bowers born March 12, 2012.
>> Kensly Bowers born July 22, 2015.
>> Finly Bowers born February 26, 2018.

DENNY: Dennis Matthew DeRose born June 27, 1959.

Spouse: Married Camilla Gay Belsher May 18, 1985.

> Kyle Riviere DeRose born February 2, 1987.
>
> Kyle married Jessica Hermina Slothouber September 17, 2016.
>> Noella DeRose born August 29, 2017.
>> Raiden DeRose born October 3, 2019.
>
> Denver Robb DeRose born April 5, 1988.
>
> Two children with Haley Cooper:
>> Austin DeRose born August 10, 2022.
>> Tate DeRose born April 30, 2024.
>
> Ryland Dennis DeRose born July 7, 1989.
>
> Ryland married Elysha Aspeslet August 19, 2017.
>> Deacon DeRose born August 4, 2018.
>> Lennie DeRose born April 2, 2020.
>
> Gavin Lloyd DeRose born December 18, 1990.
>
> Engaged to Jesse Hanson.

LULU: Charlene Cecilia DeRose born February 6, 1962.

Spouse: Married Rudy Ostrem May 19, 1991.

> Clint Ostrem, Rudy's son, born June 21, 1971.
>> Darby Ostrem born November 6, 2002.
>>> Kohen Basnett born September 13, 2022.
>> Dane Ostrem born October 11, 2004.
>> Dylann Ostrem born May 14, 2008.
>
> Toni Ostrem, Rudy's daughter, born May 12, 1972.
>> Liam Craig born May 30, 2001.
>> Sean Craig born May 17, 2008.
>
> Dawn Ostrem, Rudy's daughter, born April 15, 1974.
>> Olivia Campbell born November 14, 2014.
>
> Travis David Ostrem, Lulu and Rudy's son, born May 1, 1989.
>
> Travis married Lauren Ritchie August 9, 2014.
>> Arabella Ostrem born September 30, 2011.
>> Twins Talon David and Payton Cecilia Ostrem born May 18, 2013.
>> Rose Ostrem born June 23, 2016.

WESSEY: Rosaire Wesley DeRose born March 31, 1963. Died October 6, 1984.

Appendix 3:
Secwepemctsín Word List

Clutulucwem: Yellow Meadow or Yellow Land, the name of Cecilia's family meadow at the '18

ctsílleńten: Storehouse

Esk'et: Alkali Lake First Nation

Kúkpi7: Chief

kyé7e: Grandmother

qwllin: Birch bark

Secwepemctsín: The Secwépemc language

séme7: White person

sq̓ílye: Sweathouse

Stswecem'c Xget'tem: Dog Creek/Canoe Creek First Nation

sxúsem: Soapberry

tḱépmen: Tanning tool

t̓séllpep: Spruce roots

Tsq̓ésceň: Canim Lake First Nation

Xatśūll: Soda Creek First Nation

xpé7e: Grandfather

About the Authors

CECILIA DICK DEROSE was born into a hard-working Secwépemc family at Esk'et (Alkali Lake) on January 14, 1935. She was the fourth of ten children born to Amelia Joe and Matthew Dick, and was raised on a remote meadow a day and a half's journey by horseback from the village of Esk'et.

At seven years old, Cecilia was sent to St. Joseph's Mission, the same residential school near Williams Lake where her parents and siblings were sent. There, instead of the education she hoped would lead her to a career as a teacher, lawyer or journalist, she endured cruel treatment so familiar to those who were forced to attend residential school. Despite this, she retained her Secwepemctsín language and developed a strength of character that would carry her through the rest of her life.

After marrying a non-Indigenous man and losing her Indigenous status, Cecilia fought to retain her Secwépemc culture and traditions, and she eventually regained her status. She went on to become an ambassador of Secwépemc language and cultural practices. She eventually taught Secwepemcstín and Secwépemc culture in the public school system, fulfilling her dream of becoming a teacher.

On June 4, 2024, eighty-nine-year-old Secwépemc Elder, matriarch and knowledge keeper Cecilia Dick DeRose received an honorary doctor of letters, *honoris causa*, from Thompson Rivers University in Kamloops, BC. This prestigious recognition was bestowed upon Cecilia by her daughter DeDe DeRose, TRU's recently proclaimed chancellor, as her first official act in the role.

SAGE BIRCHWATER is the author, co-author or editor of nearly a dozen books, including *'Ulkatchot'en: The People of Ulkatcho* (Ulkatcho First Nation, 1991), *Chiwid* (New Star Books, 1995), *Gumption & Grit* (Caitlin Press, 2009), *Chilcotin Chronicles* (Caitlin Press, 2017) and *Talking to the Story Keepers* (Caitlin Press, 2022).

Sage was a journalist and rural correspondent for several newspapers and magazines, covering news and events in the Chilcotin and Bella Coola area beginning in the early 1980s. He worked as a staff writer for the *Williams Lake Tribune* from 2001 until 2009, when he retired to focus on authoring books. He lives in Williams Lake, BC, and continues to write about the Cariboo Chilcotin Central Coast region.